AESTHETICS AND APPRECIATION OF TREE TRUNKS AND BRANCHES INTO SKETCHES AND SCULPTURES

Samuel Adentwi Bentum

Publisher: Eric Kwadwo Amissah
Photographer: Ernest Doe Kudjordjie
Illustrator: Samuel Adentwi Bentum

Graphic Designers: Ernest Doe Kudjordjie And Ernest Nkrumah Taylor
Cover Page Design: Ernest Doe Kudjordjie

English Language Editor: Sam-Ackah Odeyemi
Vernacular (Fanti) Editor: Mrs. Roberta Agbeti

Printed in the United States of America.

ISBN: 978-1-4907-2118-7 (sc)
ISBN: 978-1-4907-2117-0 (hc)
ISBN: 978-1-4907-2119-4 (e)

Library of Congress Control Number: 2013922574

Trafford rev. 12/09/2013

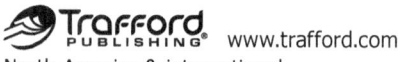 www.trafford.com
North America & international
toll-free: 1 888 232 4444 (USA & Canada)
fax: 812 355 4082

ACKNOWLEDGEMENTS

Many people helped at various stages in the production of this book. Some criticized and others encouraged the writing, but in every case I appreciate their effort. Without them I could not have achieved the publication of this book.

I cannot lose sight of Mercy Gyambea Atiemoh, Kezia Elikplim Ayanu and Elizabeth Obeng without their infectious enthusiasm and interest I never would have begun writing this book. Again I cannot gloss over the efforts of Frederick N. Anderson, Albert Ntarmah, Alex Darpoh, Abraham Boakye Amponsah and Solomon Ayeh who generously and thoughtfully took time out of their clouded schedules to interact and make constructive suggestions. Also, my sincere thanks go to Sam-Ackah Odeyemi, who painstakingly read through the manuscript and made invaluable suggestions.

Ernest Doe Kudjordjie and Ernest Nkrumah Taylor, cheerfully assisted in taking photographs of the carved pieces of the trees I used for my works and were the designers who translated the manuscripts and photographs into a book. I express my unalloyed appreciation to all those who supported me in various ways: the students of School of Applied Arts, Takoradi Polytechnic, Ghana; Bertha Mensah and Linda Essel for the careful and skilful typing of the manuscripts, Eric Kwadwo Amissah, who tactfully edited and co-ordinated the writing activity.

DEDICATION

To my mother, Madam Agnes Selina Essilfie, who has great interest in artistry.

TABLE OF CONTENTS

LIST OF PLATES

LIST OF ILLUSTRATIONS

FOREWORD

Many Africans have a bleak view of art and as a result have ignored the advantages and values thereof. However, there is enough evidence to demonstrate that the socio-cultural and political lives of Africans are affected by artists' portrayal of quality, purity and standard.

Bentum's book, *Aesthetics and Appreciation of Tree Trunks and Branches into Sketches and Sculptures* expresses his creative energy in varying dimensions. His sculptured works in the book explain some concepts that underpin African religion and magical powers – a relation of power and mystery.

Ordinarily, the works may seem strange and difficult to understand, but these sculptured pieces depict the African background replete with respect for ancestors and fear of the unseen. Bentum's collection of his sketches and sculptures shows a sense of balance and excellent treatment of surface.

Aesthetics and Appreciation of Trees Trunks and Branches into Sketches and Sculptures is the kind of book most people in Africa and elsewhere should read in order to be conversant with African art in the context of the ideals of beauty and mystery.

SAM–ACKAH ODEYEMI
(Art Critic, Dean of Students Affairs, Former Head,
Liberal Studies Department, Takoradi Polytechnic, Takoradi, Ghana.)

PREFACE

Aesthetics and Appreciation of Tree Trunks and Branches into Sketches and Sculptures introduces a way of seeing and experiencing art. For centuries, artists have relied on nature as their great source of inspiration. Tree trunks and branches are comparable natural sculpturing materials that are worthy of adoration and adoption. Nature, in this sense, directs the liberation of the images within these tree trunks and branches.

The concept, upon which these aesthetics and appreciations were deduced, was based on the philosophy of truth which presents the materials, their sources and physical appearances as the basis of these sculptures. Therefore, the need to preserve and present the material was as crucial as the artistry.

The style of these collections centred on simplified realism that clinches on plain geometric shapes and forms. Carving technique was at times interspersed with the tree bark texture, surface defects and marks from chain saw and machete. Titles of the sculptures were derived from the Akan-Fante culture and offered their English versions.

Hence, the dignity of the African culture is clearly and solidly established through the form and imagery created from these tree trunks and branches.

SAMUEL ADENTWI BENTUM (Ph.D)

INTRODUCTION

Think of this book as an academic product which has passed through several eyes and voices; imagine yours and mine, having a visual conversation and asking questions such as, what shape or what form habitate these tree trunks and branches? What is the feeling expressed? What is the message conveyed? Sometimes, the answers are far-fetched. Whether we find a particular tree trunk and branch beautiful or interesting, the competing imagery and concept may be subjective and a matter of preference. Memories, feelings, ideas, exposure and interaction are brought to bear on these works of art through nature. Nature, in this case directs the liberation of the images within the materials (tree trunks and branches).

Like the religious philosophy of 'rebirth'-giving a new life to an existing soul-the philosophy of this book is to bring back the dignity of life and restore hope through the process of exposing the various shapes, forms and images that reside in these tree trunks and branches. These tree trunks and branches are elevated from 'grass to grace'. They are provided a new identity that re-launches the African values and ethics governing individuals and communities. This new identity re-assures dignity in the form and imagery within these materials. As new found treasures and products of aesthetics, their spirits and souls are revived and lifted. In line with the African philosophy of survival, growth and continuity of life, the tree trunks and branches were picked from their respective locations (soil, street sides, backyards, construction sites etc) and offered the needed attention and treatment. They assumed the new and real life like any community member.

Nature and her attributes have for centuries become the source of inspiration for artists. Nature suggests to artists varied shapes, forms, textures, colours, and other things that dwell in her. It is undeniable that nature as an inspirational medium deals bountifully with artistic creation in realism and non-realism representations. The individual tree trunks and branches provide clues to the varied subject matter and concepts. Human forms and details appear as knots, grooves, slots, and protrusions which lead artists to craft features such as eyes, nose, mouth, breast, and other parts in a fascinating manner.

As a meaningful contribution to the world of art, this book seeks to address the issue of environmental cleaning in another dimension. Nature continually inspire artists to undertake environmental cleaning through careful selection of materials (tree trunks and branches) as raw materials for art production. Although these tree trunks and branches are scientifically taken care of by nature as a bio-degradable materials, their continuous stay on the street side and backyards is hazardous to humanity. They may also serve as abodes to reptiles and lunatics. They have gradually become a point of convergence for today's menace caused by plastic waste. Therefore their identification and collection as raw materials for art production may by itself serve as a mode of cleaning the environment as well as preventing it from becoming the collection point for fly up and light weight non-degradable waste.

It is hoped that this book would suggest to nature artists to organize regular pilgrimage to nearby wood-lands to look for the possibility of offering them exposure in identifying the creativity within nature which is needed to galvanize nature art presentation and environmental preservation. The twists and turns, regular and irregular forms, smooth and tactile surface textures, end-splits and cracks, pin-holes and rotten portions presented to humanity by these tree trunks and branches are worthy of art production and adoration.

Tree trunks and branches offer artists another dimension of material base and also a search into the use of lesser patronized exotic species of trees that hitherto have little admiration to wood workers. It is perceptual that art (sculpture) production and their adjunct conceptualization will contribute to the restoration of the fading African values and ethics. These art pieces serve as a mode of expressing the precious *Africaness* needed to keep sanity and security in the community.

All the sculptures in this book bear Akan titles with their English translations. The titles were all drawn from everyday life and the underlying concepts constitute their individual compositions. Akan, as seen in this book, refers to the group of ethnic people found on West Coast of Africa South of the Sahara. They include groups such as Guans, Buems, Fantes, Akwapims, Asantes, Nzemas, Fafras, of Ghana and Baules of Ivory Coast. For the purpose of this book, the term Akan makes reference to only the Fantes from the Central Region in Ghana.

The tree used in the production of these carved pieces of tree trunks and branches is Senna Siamea. Senna Siamea, also known as Kassod tree or Cossod tree, is a legume in the sub-family. Senna Siamea is an exotic tree that has a coppicing property. Again it is an amity plant used to decorate and beautify compounds and streets or road sides. This tree accommodates crop production since it is planted alongside other crops. Senna Siamea is also an agro-forestry tree that was introduced to Central Region, Ghana, at the Brimso Water Headworks as wood fuel to generate energy to turn turbines. It was planted around the water body as vegetation cover. Senna Siamea was adopted and planted along streets and roads for the purpose of beautification and a source of shade to pedestrians. It has since been adopted by Forestry Commission as wood fuel for charcoal production. This was to reduce the reliance on timber as a source of fuel.

Senna Siamea is found mostly in Thailand, Arabia, and part of tropical Africa. The leaves, pods and seeds are edible but after thorough boiling. Senna Siamea contains a chemical compound *Baraboi* which is used in traditional herbal medicine. This chemical possesses sedative and anxiolytic properties. The mature Senna Siamea tree has a diameter of approximately seventy centimeters and a compact grain that makes it an extremely hard wood that tends to damage the cutting edge of metal tools. It has a beautiful dark grain pattern and a pale yellow sap.

Senna Siamea contains tannin that makes the wood stony when exposed to the sun ray. It has not been introduced to furniture production but is popular in wood carving. Both the pole structure and the multiple protrusions with twists, turns, bends, knots, dents and grooves are used for carving. These come with varied diameters, lengths and colours that range from pale yellow to burnt umber or off black. Depending on the source of the material, end splits, surface cracks, pin holes, decays, burns and machete marks feature prominently on the tree trunks and branches. These make the sculptures to assume character and dynamism.

A correlation of naturalism and cubism form the foundation of the style of artistry. Simplified realism in plain geometric rendition dominates the production. The entire collection manifests a parallel of natural forms and carving. Carving techniques are employed on all the pieces. This involves the use of gouges and chisels as well as handsaw and electric powered chainsaw. The saws are used to create the initial forms and shapes and to level the base of the tree trunks and branches. Large-sized gouges and chisels are used to evolve the initial shapes and forms into the images. Small and medium-sized gouges and chisels are used for details and features of the images. Mild grade of sand paper is run over the pieces to blunt all available wood burrs before chemical finish is applied.

Gouge-cut pattern runs through the entire collection. Conscious impression of small and large cuts of 'C'-gouges are produced. The gouge patterns are in some instances interspersed with the tree bark texture and surface defects resulting from natural phenomena and pests. Marks are created from chain saw and machete as part of human action either consciously or unconsciously. These marks then become artificially formed features on the tree trunks and branches and create impressions on variety of surface treatments. All the carved pieces are first coated with petroleum fluid (diesel or gas oil) which has the property that kills wood worms and insects and also provides a mellow shin on the surface of the pieces. This is repeated to ensure effective protection of the pieces since diesel has the potency to protect wood. It also served as sealant to the wood and makes the sculptures water-resistive and become conducive for outdoor display. These tree trunks and branches promote aesthetic appreciation of thoughts and perception in art.

ADZEPA Yε NA
(A TREASURE THAT IS HARD TO FIND)

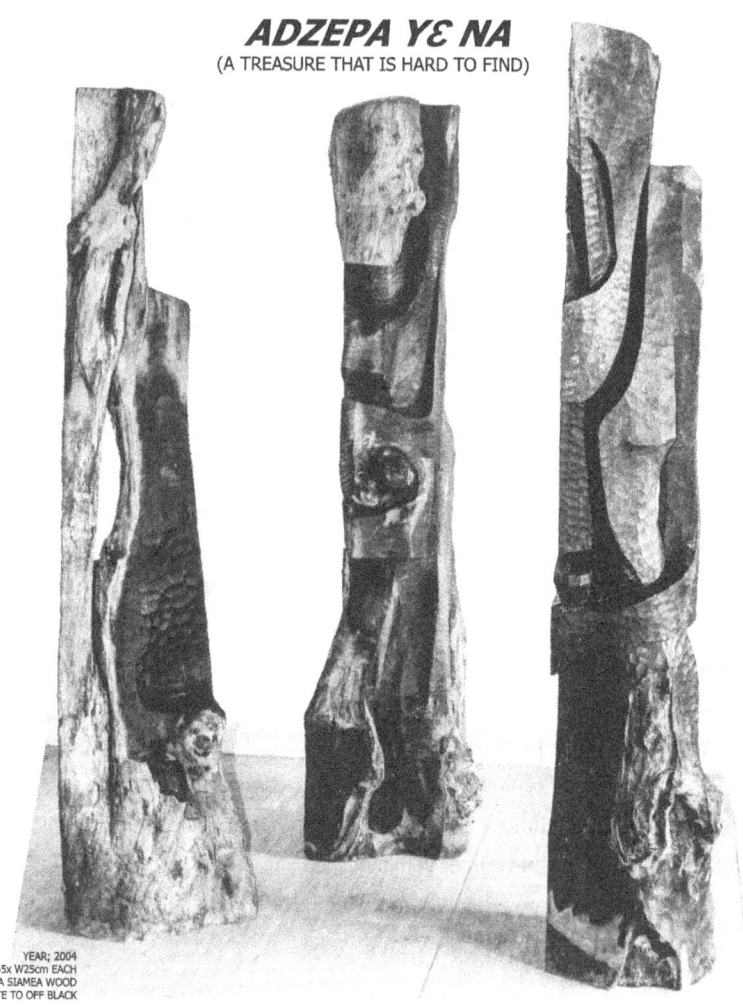

YEAR; 2004
DIMENSION: H165x L45x W25cm EACH
MEDIUM: SENNA SIAMEA WOOD
COLOUR: OFF WHITE TO OFF BLACK

Adzepa Yɛ Na in Akan language literally connotes *a Treasure that is Hard to Find.* In the Akan culture, adolescent females and males are expected to keep their purity until customary marriage is contracted on their behalf. Therefore, the youth are not supposed to be carnally seeing their opposite sex. To the African, sex as an act is the preserve of the legally married persons only. Persons, who are outside the marriage group but are found indulging in sex act are punished. Also, it is unacceptable for both females and males to indulge in multiple relationships.

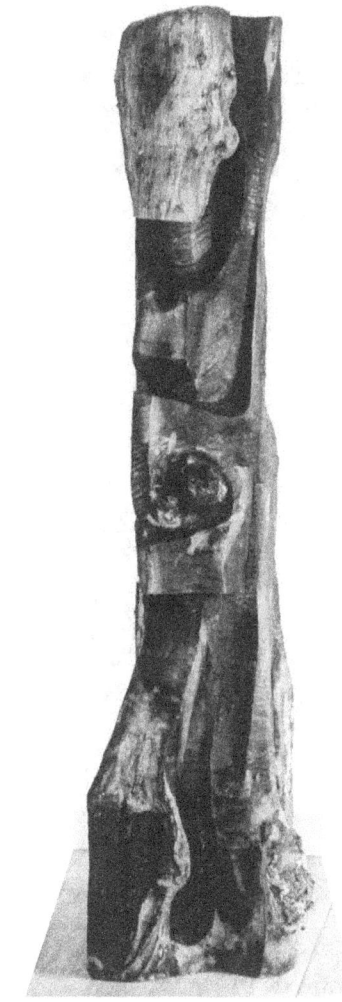

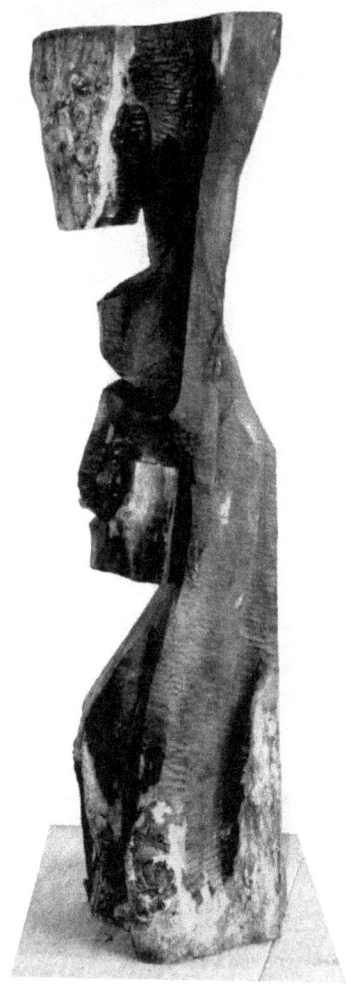

Such persons are never commended for marriage. When persons with such character do marry, they are seen by the society as adulterous. Additionally, the Akan culture totally rejects marriage among females and also between males since such act is regarded as taboo. With the influx of other cultures from non-African background, promiscuity and infidelity among the youth and adult have become common and in vogue. Therefore, this composition seeks to reiterate this African value.

Adzepa yɛ na is a three-piece composition that consists of a female and two males, produced from three separate wood poles. These lend themselves to a realistic sculpture rendition. All the three pieces may be arranged or positioned to the viewers according to their wish and space. The composition displays equal sizes of tree bark and carved portion. The female figure that has a faceless head is posed in a pouring posture evident of her service to men (victims - two male figures). She is fully modelled to fit the contemporary style of form and surface treatment of Western and African academicism.

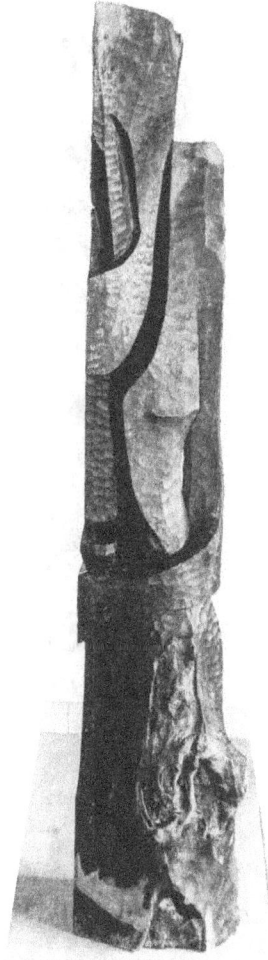

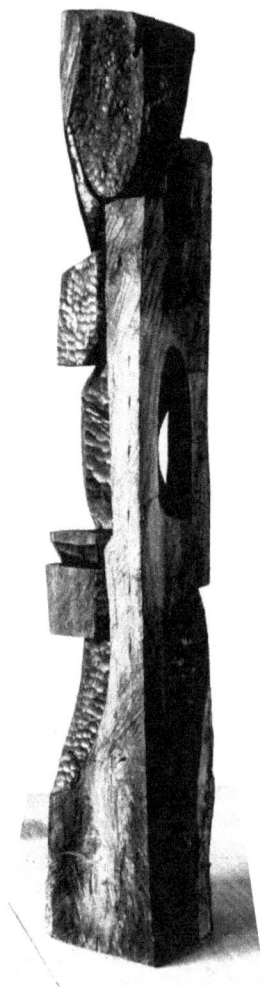

The first male figure has also been rendered in the contemporary style of form and surface treatment of Western and African academicism. This figure is faceless and its head is turned backward. The left hand holds an almost full calabash (wine bowl) that is positioned across the abdomen (stomach) while the right hand is placed on the right side of the figure.

The second male figure is composed from two poles that are fused at the top and bottom portions. This figure has a greater portion of its surface uncarved. The left pole represents the torso, while the right one stands for the hand that holds the calabash that is ready to receive the wine. The figure has one large eye and a small eye. It has a long wrecked nose and an opened carved mouth.

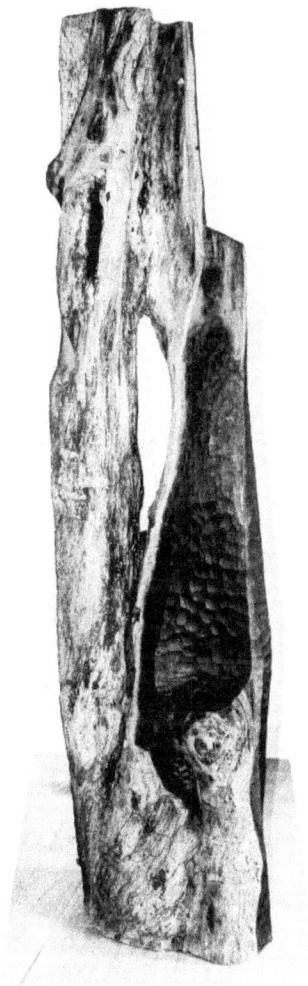

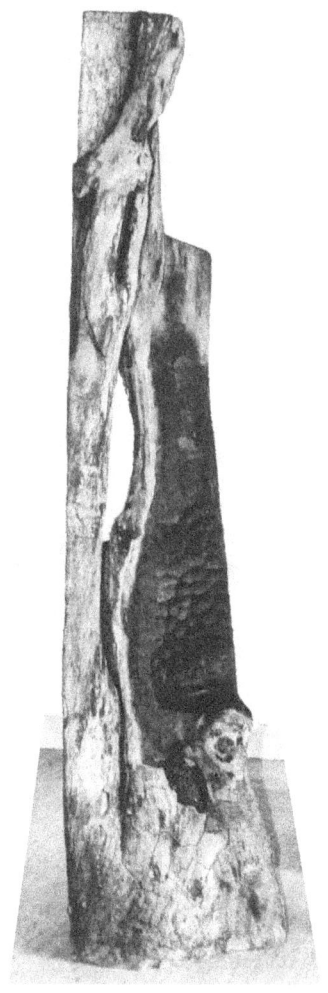

All these features set the face in an elongated posture. It therefore provides the face with a fearful mood. The top portion of this figure has a display of decay and termite infestation, but the bottom portion reveals a crack and flick of a weak tree bark.

CONCEPT

Adzepa yɛ na is a multi-composition that addresses the immoral aspect of the youth in our community. The African culture frowns on women dating more than one man or engaging in extra-marital relationship. In today's culture, females have dual and multi-relations according to their taste in terms of acculturation, westernization, modernization and love culture.

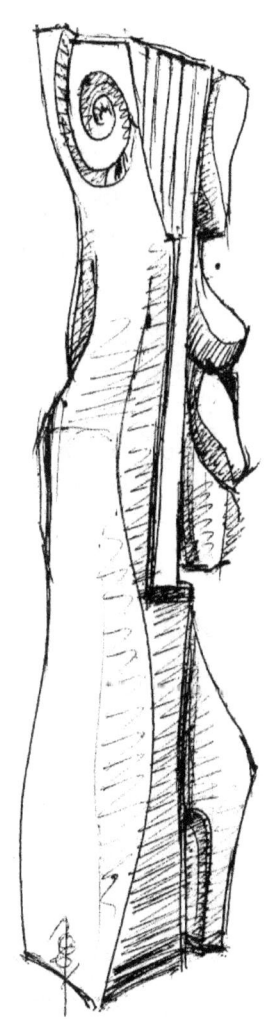

13

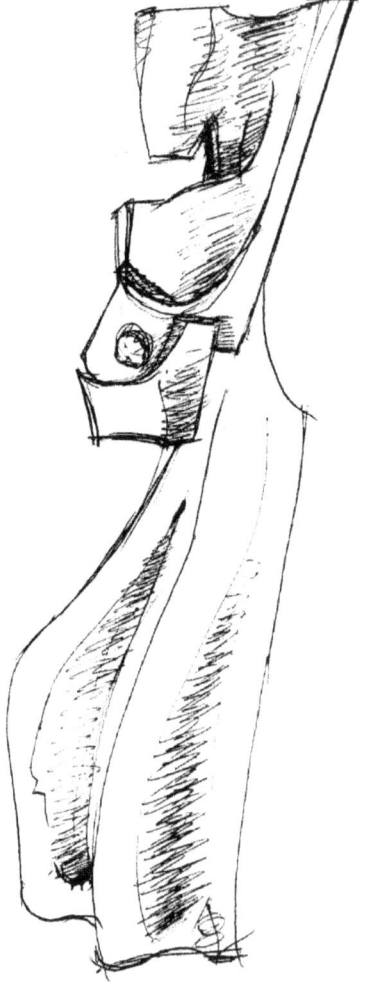

Adzepa yɛ na projects a female youth gracefully serving two males simultaneously without the men knowing their predicament and vulnerability to her promiscuousness.

The wine represents the excessive desire of a woman's treasures by men regardless of the filth it may come with her hidden, shameful act within the faceless head that also contains decay that symbolizes the evil and deceit of her life style.

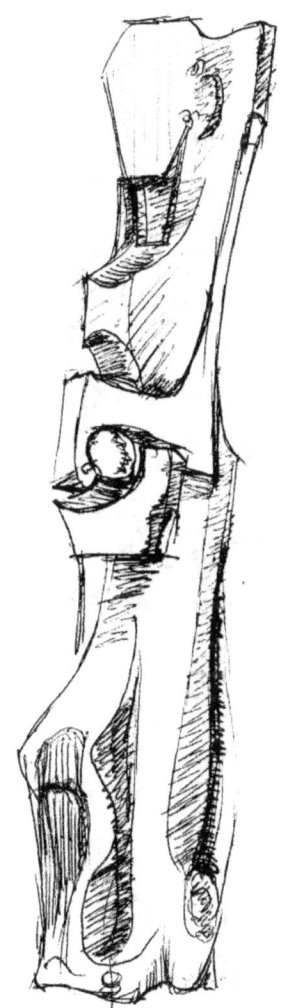

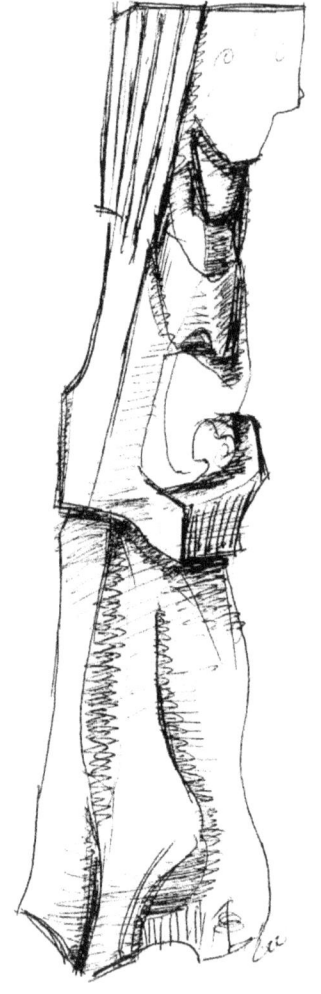

The modelled part of this female figure represents the contemporariness and modernist imitations that have taken over the preservation of the virtues of the African culture and African value that prohibit promiscuity and immorality among the female gender. The first male figure is offered the same contemporariness and modernist presentation as that of the female.

There is the general belief that the western civilization is worth embracing but has the tendency to unduly influence people. Therefore, the faceless-turned-male figurehead represents a group of men who are ever ready to subject themselves to the abuse and unfaithfulness of women, even when confronted with wisdom, guilt and the will of God.

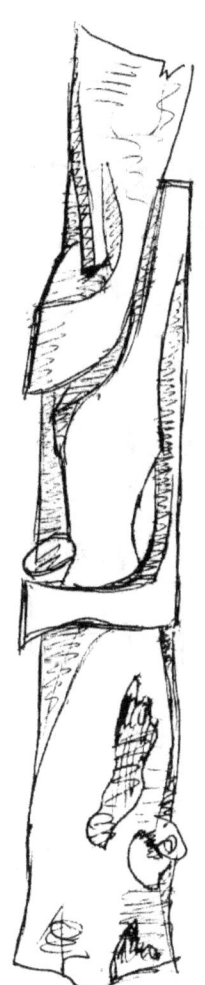

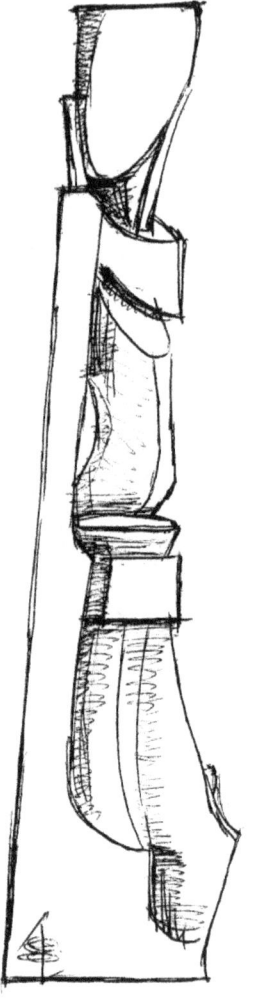

They are carnal and will not attempt resisting the attraction of women. They are ready to go in for anything that is feminine. The male holds in his hands a fully filled calabash that connotes wealth, will and attraction which empowers him to infiltrate into the female world. He represents the moral decadence of the community. His soul and being are longing for self-destruction and self-satisfaction rather than the will of God.

The second male represents the type of men who are always confronted with shock, fear, dismay and disappointment from females yet prefer to live their lives with such predicament. The large eye of the art piece positioned in the tree bark mirrors his inability to identify the challenges and problems associated with relationship. Like the Akan adage *wo enyiwa soso a nna ɔnnkyerɔ dɛ ihu adze* literally meaning *big eye does not connote factual perception.*

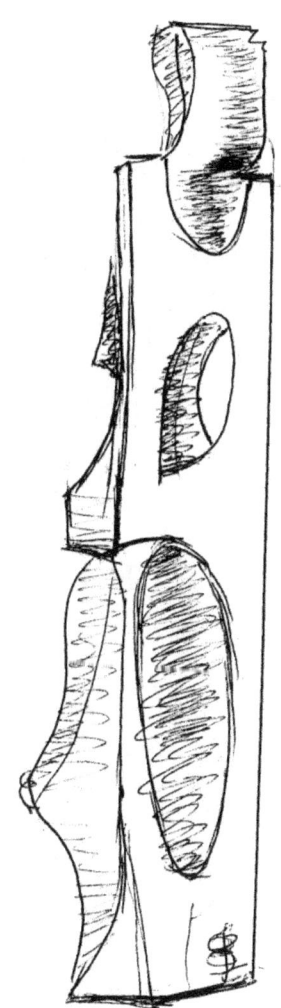

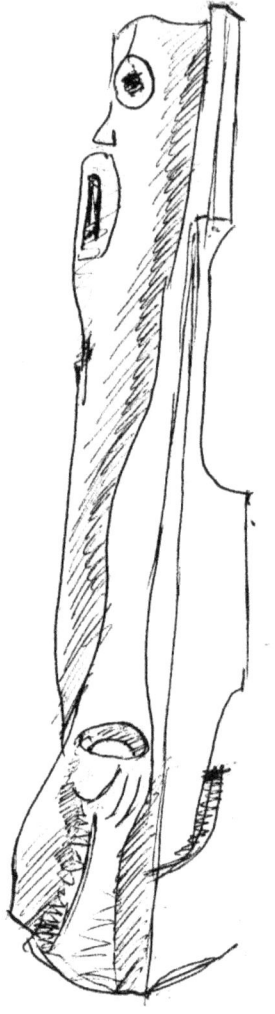

The wrecked nose in the image represents the male's inability to smell the filth that surrounds him, in spite of all the deadly and fearful sicknesses that afflict men. The largely opened mouth portrays the shocks that confront him upon the sight of his unfaithful mistress. The large portion of the rotten and uncarved areas identified his ignorance, social and financial misfits and mental deficiencies. This represents the man's inability to display his calabash vividly before the community.

This composition seeks to advise adolescent females and males to keep their purity for a better future. It also admonishes women to be faithful and upright in their relations while men are encouraged to keep one partner so that they can avoid confrontation in relationship and wastage in their spendings in real life.

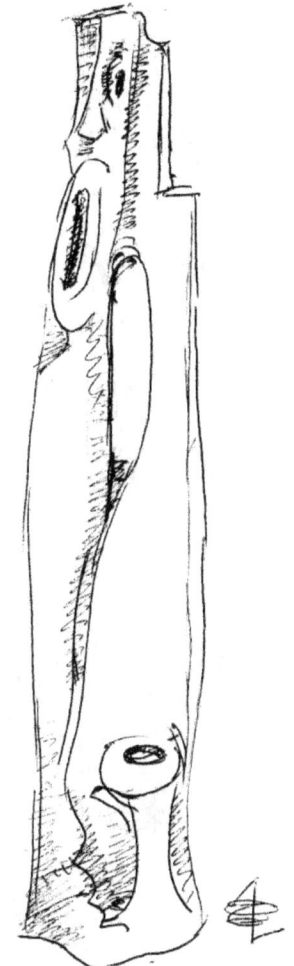

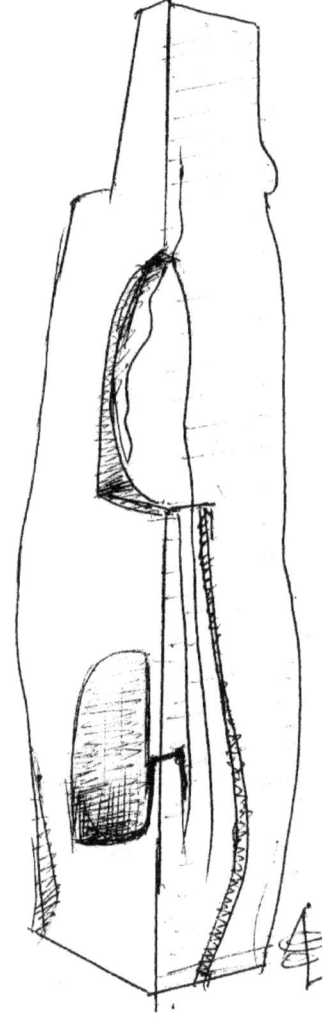

If a relationship becomes better, peace prevails. The adherence to such moral values will make a person able to stand out as a role model in the community, hence the adage; *Adzepa yɛ na* which connotes *Adzepa na ɔtɔn no ho* literally implying *a precious treasure markets itself.*

AHYƐSE MU Wɔ EWIE
(BEGINNING OF THE END)

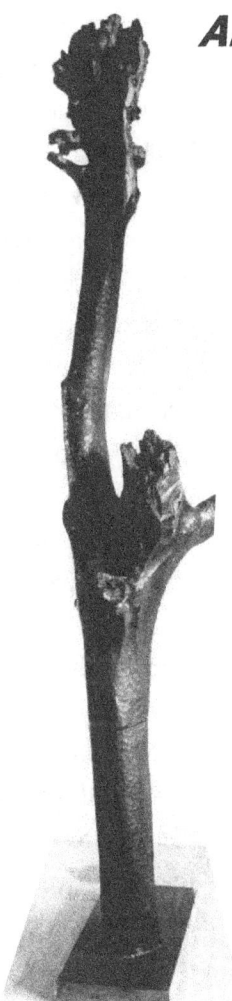

YEAR; 2005
DIMENSION: H240 x L50 x W50cm
MEDIUM: SENNA SIAMEA WOOD
COLOUR: PALE YELLOW AND BURNT UMBER

23

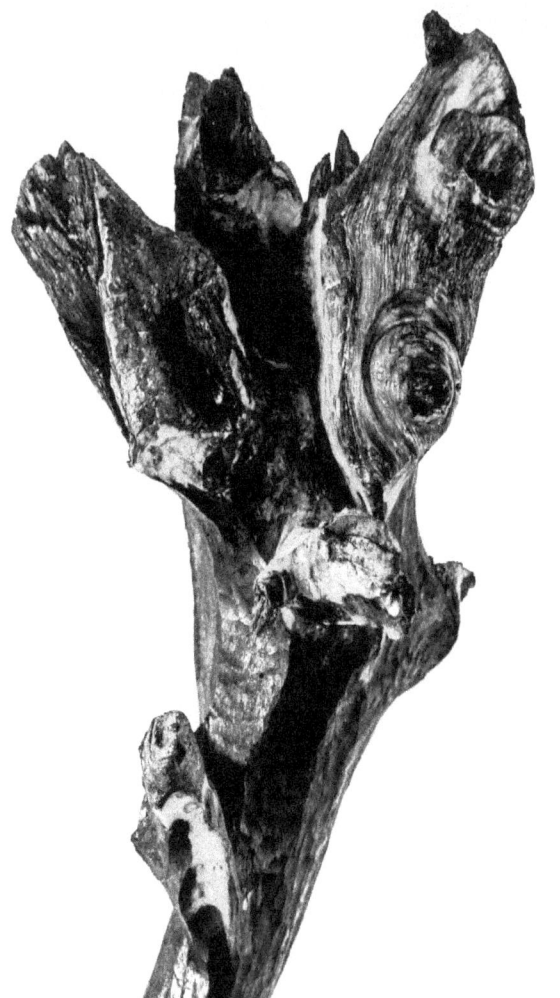

At outdooring and naming ceremonies the child is lifted up to show appreciation to the spirit world. In Africa, all newly born children are celebrated because an ancestor has once again chosen the path to the physical world. This signifies the end of the spirit (Unseen) world and the beginning of the human (Seen) world. *Ahyɛse Mu Wɔ Ewie*, in Akan literally means *Beginning of the End*. The Akan culture approves the African philosophy of reincarnation which presumes that all newly born children are the reappearances of ancestors. Based on this belief, children are named after ancestors so that they take on the character and spirit of these ancestors.

24

Ahyɛse mu wɔ ewie is a composition of an adult male performing an out-dooring and naming ceremony of a newly born child. In this composition, a male adult is seen presenting the new child to the supernatural forces: Almighty God, deities, ancestors and other benevolent family spirits who might have offered the parents their great blessing, that is the child. This pole sculpture is made from a tree trunk that is projected at the mid-section and the top section. The composition demonstrates a full rendition of gouge finishing.

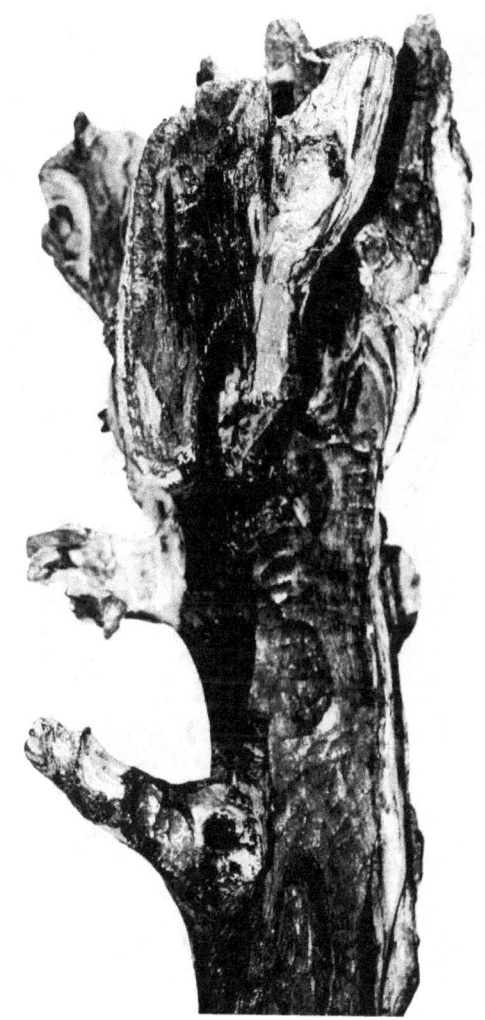

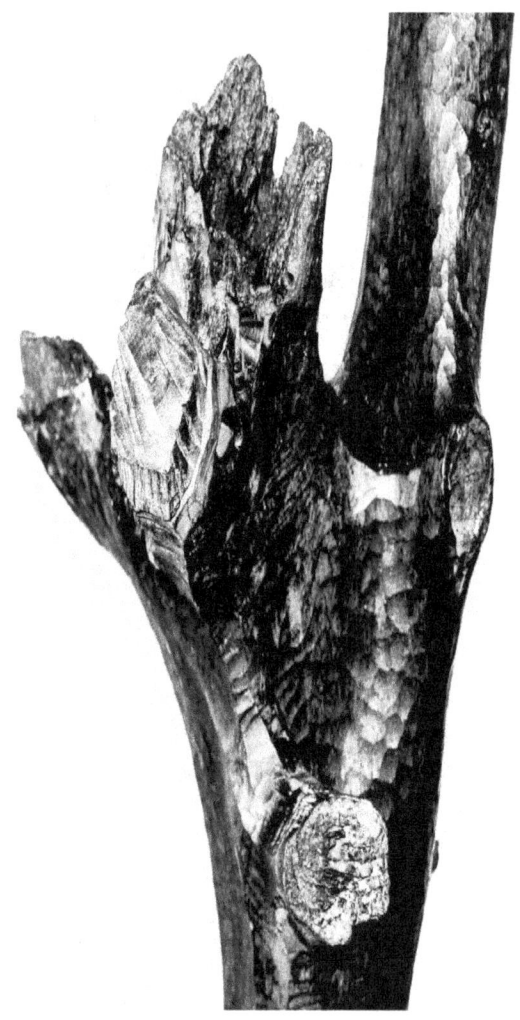

The figure's right upper arm is raised high, holding the child. The head is also raised towards the sky. The mouth is widely opened. This was created out of a natural depression and was represented as part of the head. The top portion of the composition has evidence of the tree back and sap offshoots and defect that suggest the hand is holding the child. It is only the head of the child that is showing and that the body is wrapped by the tree bark and the right hand.

The left upper arm has been stretched towards the top back of the figure in a folded pattern. The figure is dressed in the Akan casual apparel for males, that is, a piece of cloth is wrapped around the waist but drips towards the legs. This is indicated by the horizontal line that separates the top of the figure from the lower portion. The wrapped cloth does not suggest any form of drapery. The composition is planted in a rectangular wooden block that serves as the base and produces the pole sculpture with stability.

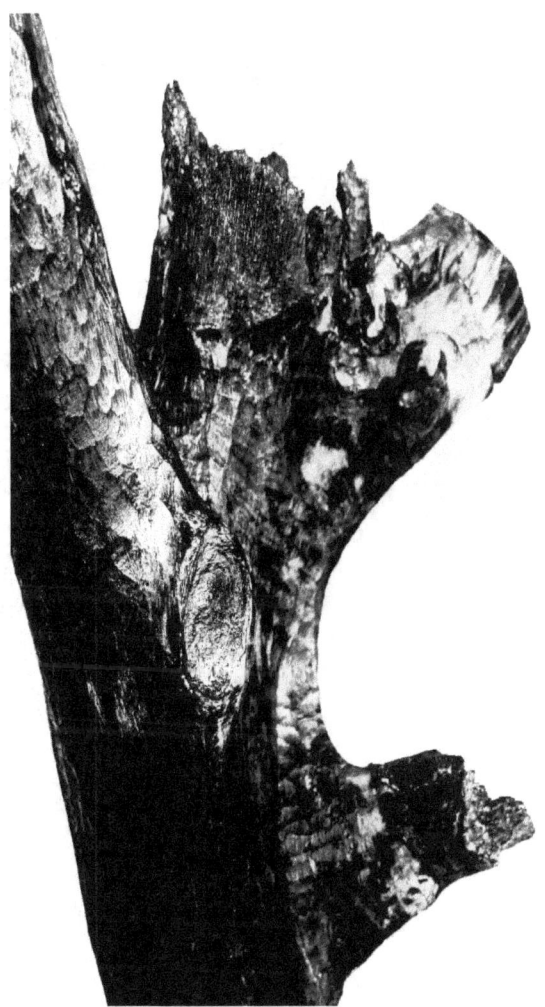

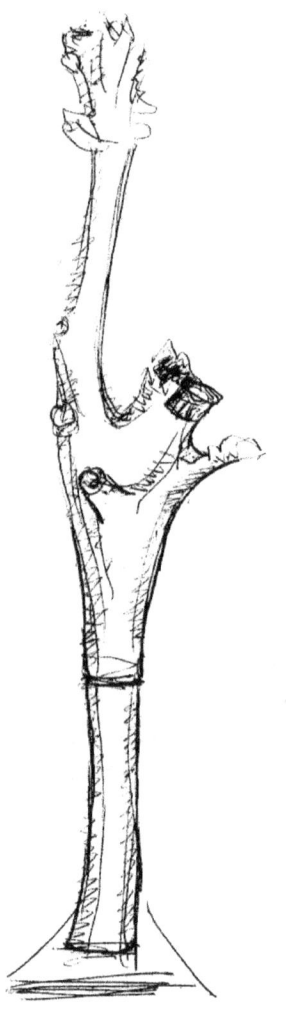

CONCEPT

Ahyɛse mu wɔ ewie offers reverence and thanks to Almighty God, deities, ancestors, and other benevolent family spirits for providing the community with a child. It also seeks to thank the ancestors for offering themselves to come back to the physical world as living beings in order to help satisfy the needs of the community upon the request of the living. To the African, pregnancy is a mystery, since it is the period when ancestors are entreated to volunteer themselves to reappear in the physical world as children. The Akans believe that a child belongs to the entire community, but not just for the biological parents. Hence, the need for the celebration of pregnancy, birth and the child by the entire community.

The Akan male casual apparel - the piece of cloth wrapped around the waist, with its non-drapery nature and the horizontal line representing the non-elaborate form of the folded cloth around the waist symbolizes the act of humility and sober appearance before the ancestors. The child's body wrapped by the tree bark symbolizes the mystery that surrounds pregnancy and child birth- a hidden process that is beyond human understanding, and a process through which the Unseen choose to become Seen. The raised head and the widely opened mouth of the male figure symbolize the act of offering reverence to the Creator, the deities and the ancestors for the gift of the child.

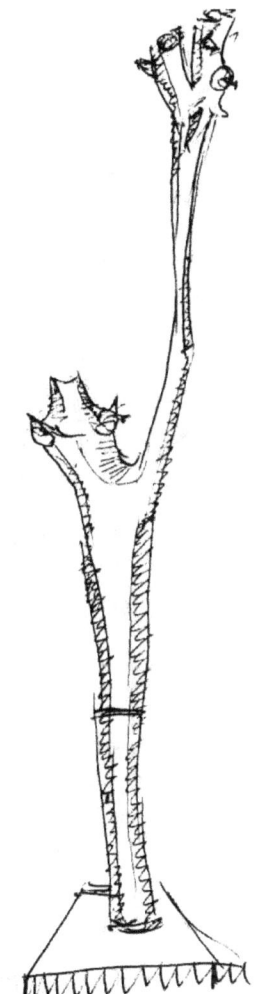

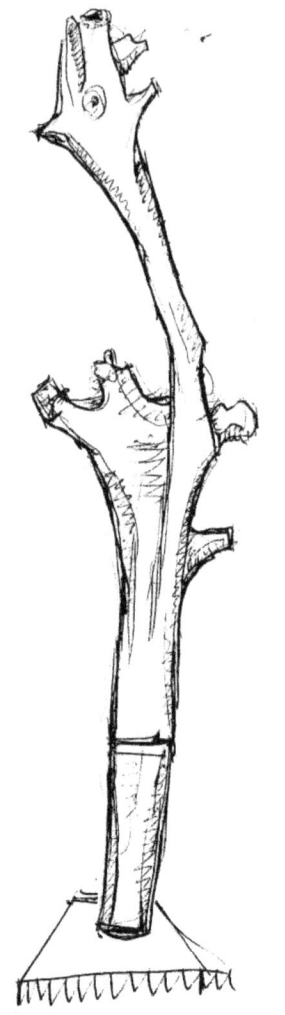

The African belief in the Philosophy of Reincarnation means all new children are born as a result of the reappearance of a dead relation or ancestor. By this belief all newly born children are named after one dead relative or the other. This therefore allows the dead to rejoin the living through birth. It therefore behoves on the living to offer reverence and thanks to the spirit world for their assistance and support. Hence, there is the need to appreciate the relationship between the living and the spirit worlds in life.

BƆM SANKU
(PLAY ME SOME MUSIC FROM MUSICAL GADGET)

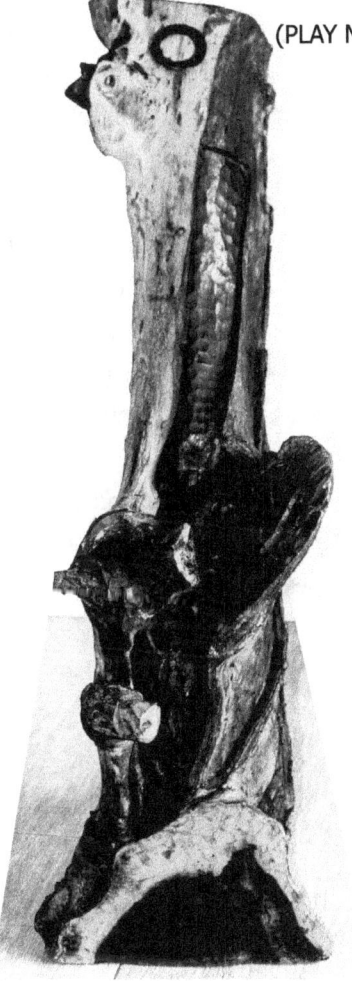

YEAR; 2005
DIMENSION: H150 x L70 x W50cm
MEDIUM: SENNA SIAMEA WOOD
COLOUR: PALE YELLOW AND BURNT URMBER

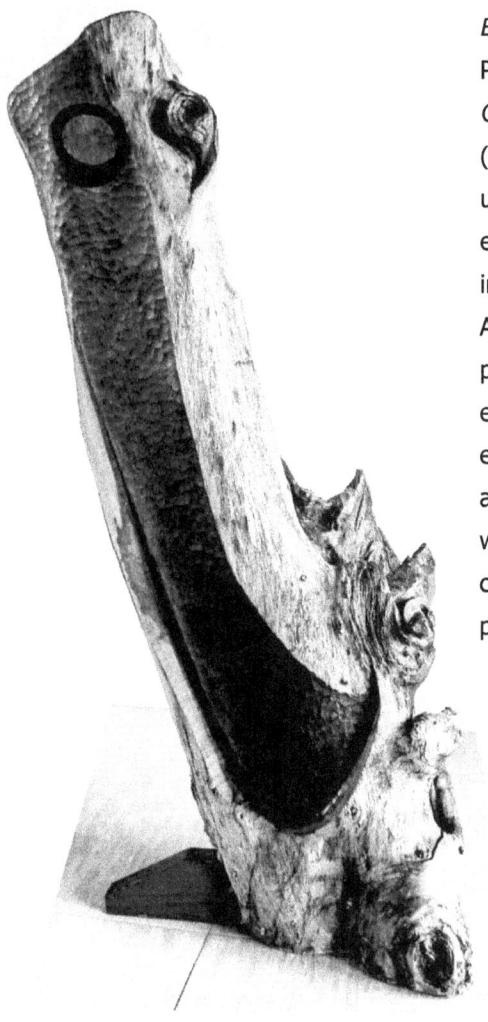

Bɔm Sanku in Akan literally means *Play Me Some Music From Musical Gadget*. In the Akan culture, *'Sanku'* (guitar) is a musical cord instrument used as a means to tell stories, entertain and provide advice to individuals and the community. The African believes that the performance of music, to a greater extent, emphasises the harmony that exists between humans and the animal world the Seen and Unseen worlds. The Seen and Unseen worlds complement each other to create peace and harmony.

Bɔm Sanku is a composition of an adult male playing guitar music and singing as well. This is a seated figure that leans backwards. The guitarist has spread his legs across the foreground. He is in a twisted pose. The composition is produced from a twisted tree branch that displays the tree bark at the back of the figure and the bottom portion. The composition exhibits projected nuts and grooves that are found at the top front representing the twisted nose and mouth and the bottom ones representing the hands and feet.

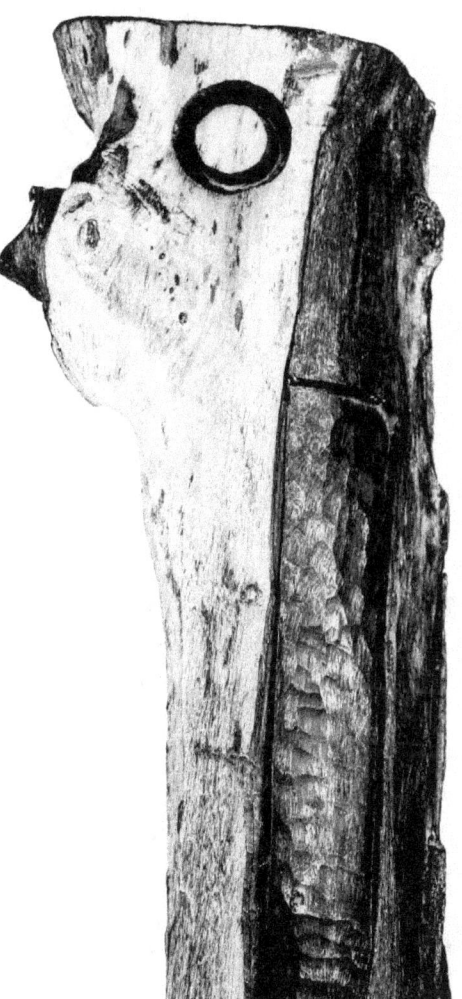

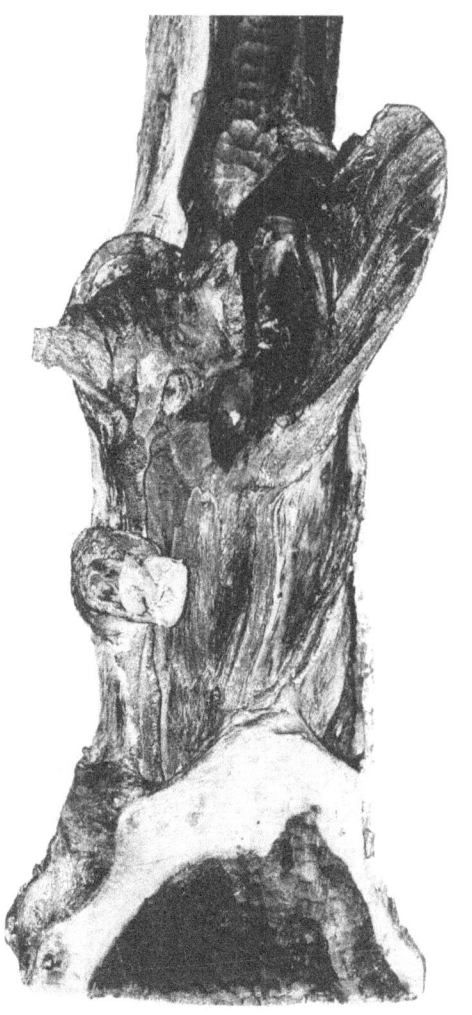

The groove in the upper nut represents a singing mouth while the right bottom nut represents the hand pulling the guitar strings. The left projection represents the hands pressing and releasing the guitar strings. The large groove stretching from the area between the hands to the feet represents the opening of the guitar box. The figure is perceived to be wearing a cloak. The composition presents a greater portion of the natural cover of the tree branch. Very little of the wood is carved. These carved portions are found around the eyes, the right side and the front portion that represent the fret of the musical instrument. The said carved portions present the rich grain patterns that inhabit the acacia wood. These rich grain patterns create a sweet interplay between carved portions and that of the natural bark of the tree branch.

CONCEPT

This composition represents the harmony that exists in the African community where the Seen or the living take care of the Unseen or Spirit world and the Unseen provide the Seen with their material and spiritual needs. To the African, the spirit world is as vibrant as the world of the living. They complement each other. The Seen constitute all living persons. The Unseen comprise Almighty God, deities, spirits of the environment, ancestors and other spirits. The upper portion of the composition (the head) represents the living. This includes bulging eyes which, though wide but cannot see beyond the physical world. Opened nose and mouth that are used to perceive or feel the presence of the spirit world and offer praises

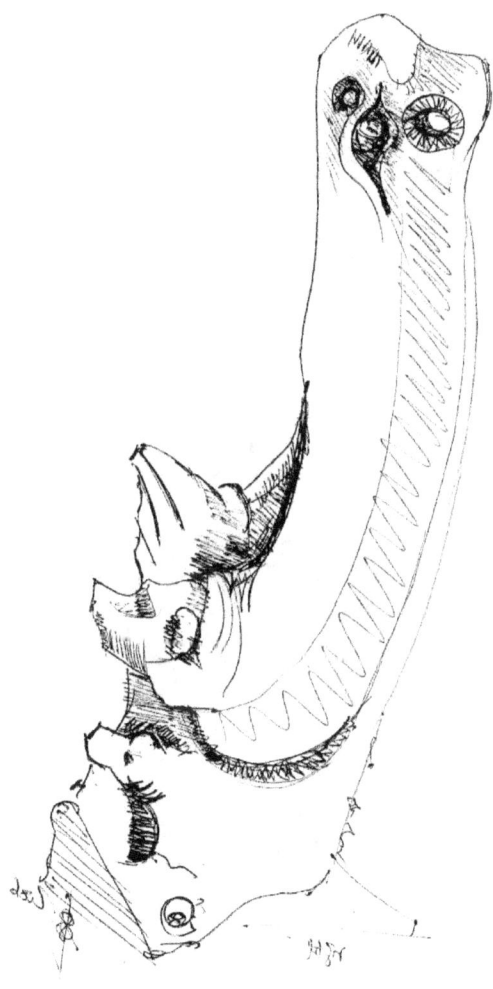

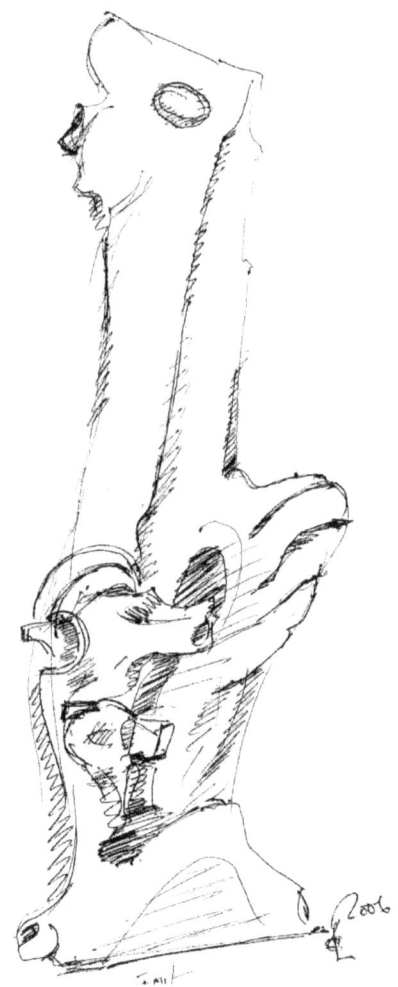

and reverences to these supernatural powers for providing them their needs and security. The lower portion of the composition represents the spirit world. The anthropomorphic figures represent that hand that is used to pull and press the guitar strings to create music. The hand pulling the string is represented by the head of a tiger while the hand pressing the string is represented by the wing of a bird. The knob used to tie the string is made from the head of the lion. These creatures represent the spiritual powers of animals (their presence in the composition forms part of the spirit world. The spirit world controls the physical world hence their appearance in the composition).

When the Seen continuously disregard the prescriptions and dictates of the Unseen, chaos and calamity befall them. Also, when the Unseen are noted to be persistently unable to respond to the plea of the Seen, it leads to their eventual neglect and abandonment. There is therefore the need for their co-existence to facilitate peace and growth within the individuals and the community. *Bɔm Sanku na bɔ ne dɛɛdɛw* is an Akan adage that literally means *play me some sweet music from your musical device*. The performance of the guitar music, to a greater extent emphasises the harmony that exists between the living world and that of the spirit world. The Seen and Unseen worlds complement and create peace and harmony.

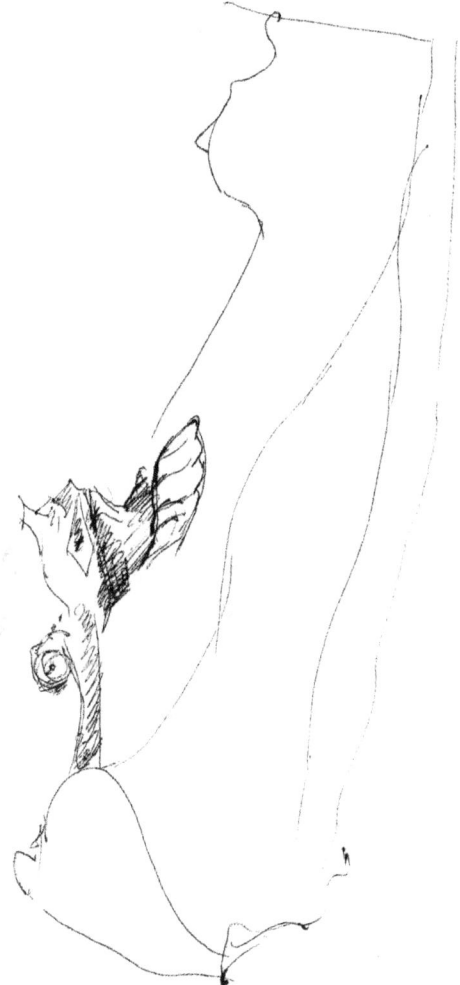

BRAGOR
(PUBERTY)

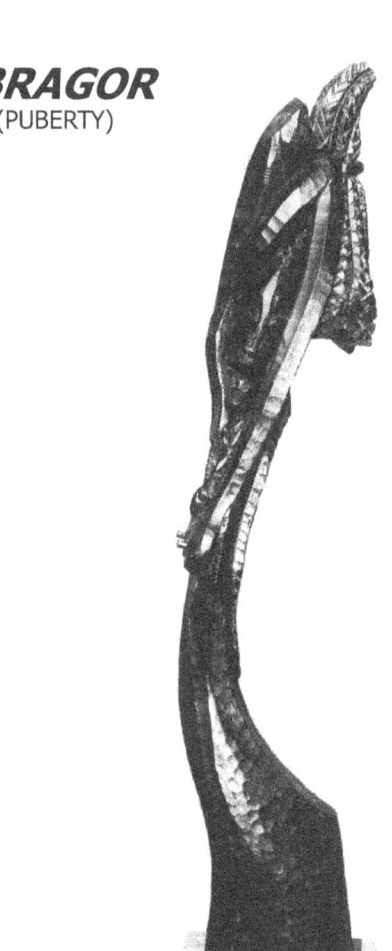

YEAR; 2004
DIMENSION: H105 x L30 x W 25cm
MEDIUM: SENNA SIAMEA WOOD
COLOUR: JET BLACK

38

Bragor in Akan language literally means *Puberty*. The Akan culture applauds purity and vitality of an adolescent as a beacon of hope for herself and the community. The African believes that the youth who are the future leaders of the community must keep themselves pure and holy. The belief is that purity must be the hallmark of every adolescent who aspires to be a faithful and fruitful partner. Therefore, evidence of sanctity, purity and virginity of a bride at first intercourse is a mark of good childhood and nurturing. The adolescent who indulges in carnal act and is promiscuous is punished. The future of such a person is ruined and as a result shame, curses and financial levies imposed on her. The culprits may also lose their pride of womanhood since they risk being recommended for marriage. Servitude is the preserve of the African.

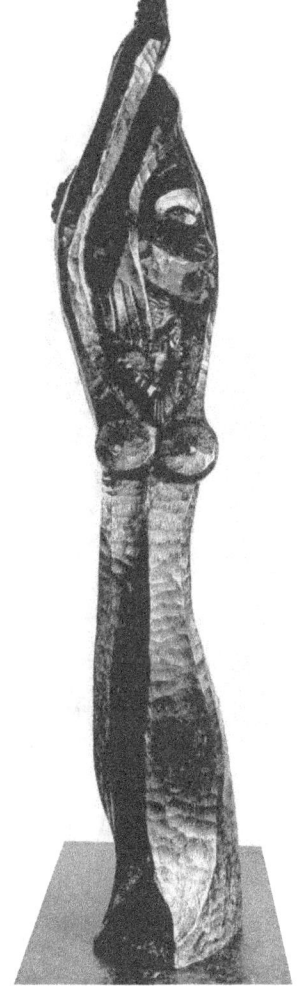

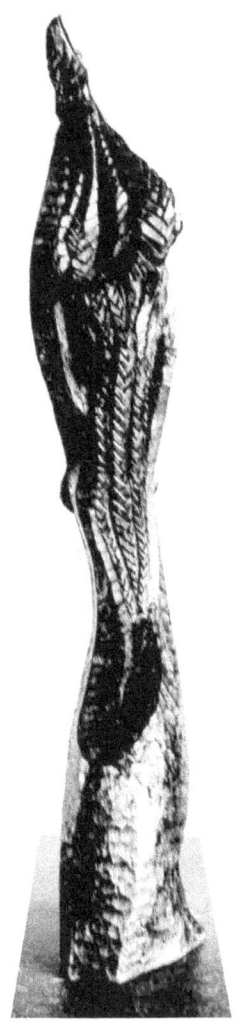

Bragor is composed of an adolescent female in a bend - forward posture. This is a semi–nude figure with underdeveloped breasts that bear a firm but long and piercing nipples. The composition is produced from a tree branch. The figure is composed from the head to the upper thigh. She has an elongated head, torso and arms. The elongated head has been encapsulated from the front and back by the upper part of the arms, therefore leaving the face to appear lean in front. The lean face projects an Akan traditional fertility mask used at puberty.

The head wears an elaborate coiffure that protrudes on the top and the back of the head. The strings of the coiffure take their root from the base of the back of the head that flows down the spine of the figure. Both elbows of the arms are stretched high up and are interlaced with the elaborate coiffure seen at the top and back of the head. The hands and fingers are positioned downwards and are found on both sides of the head. *Bragor* is a perfect rendition of the adolescent female.

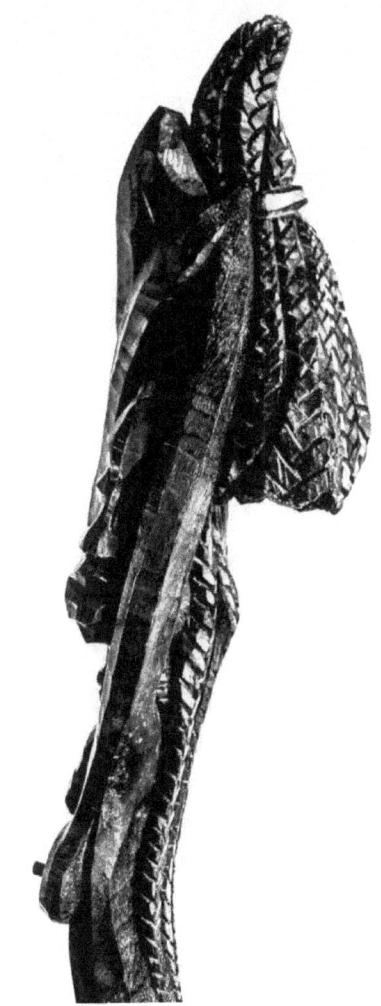

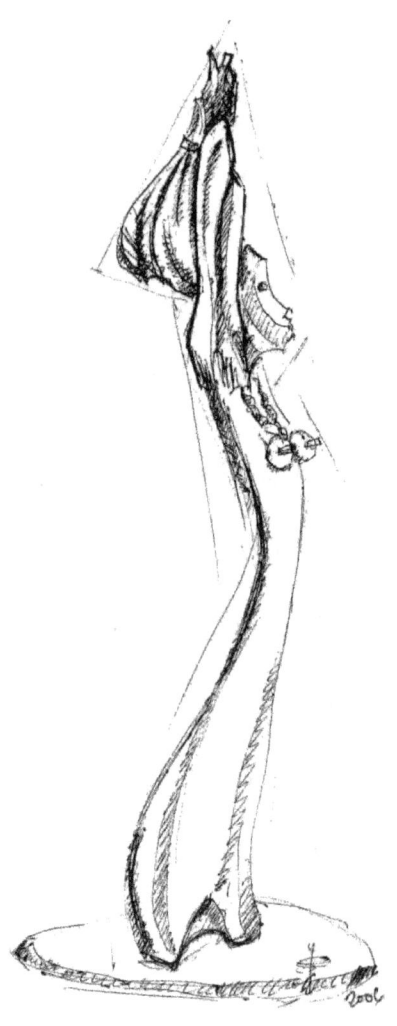

CONCEPT

Bragor is a symbol of sanctity, purity, vitality and a beacon of hope for her community. The composition informs and educates today's youth and the community at large on the importance of keeping oneself for dignity and progress. She projects the symbol of growth, survival and continuity of the individual, family and community. The African philosophy requires of her indigenes to start, continue, and finish up with the destiny bestowed on her. Because females are the torch bearers of the present and future generations, the hope for their communities resides in them. It is therefore essential that females keep their vitality for continuity of the generations to come. The pride of purity dwells in decency. The elongated figure signifies the endurance and undue stress that exist as a result of social dictates and demands.

The elaborate coiffure that sits on the head symbolises the glooming and blooming nature of a bud of flower, a symbol of hope and a better tomorrow. Puberty is therefore the hope for the next generation. The semi–nude figure presents the uncovered treasure of the human race, a potentiality that is yet to be discovered. The immature breasts reflect the possible human resources that exist within the youth but remain untapped. To the African, [the female breasts assure that the community that human nourishes available to protect and promote the human race.], it is not socially ripe for use since sex is a taboo to the unmarried. The female breasts assure the community of the protection and promotion of human nourishment in the years to come in the community.

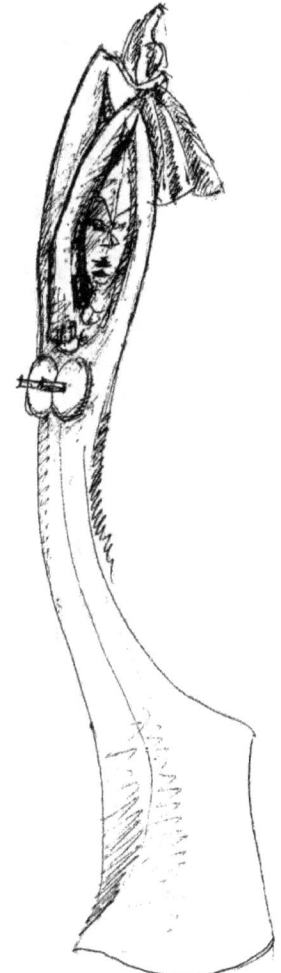

43

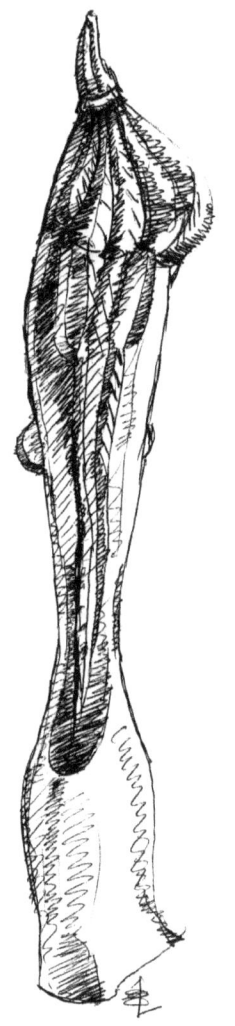

Notwithstanding, the firm but long and piercing nipples assure the community of the possible sexual attraction and pleasure that can be upheld at a more convenient time. The non-representation of the legs and the details on the upper portion of the lower arms demonstrates one of the qualities that abound in the life of the youth. Since one cannot predict the future of the youth, it is prudent to wait until one has reasonably made good strides in their life. Therefore, keeping oneself from social and moral dictates and demands is a necessity for progress.

ƆBRAGU
(DESPAIR)

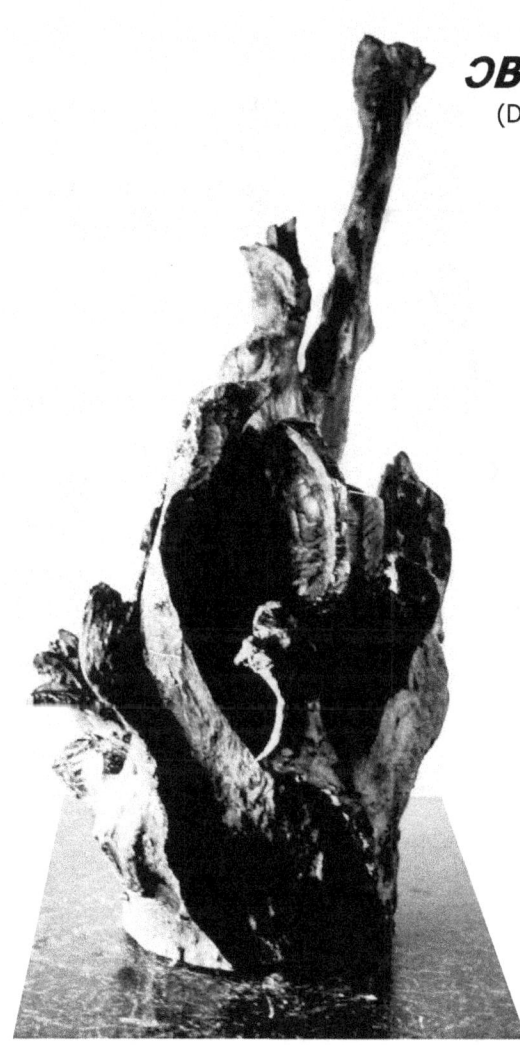

YEAR; 2005
DIMENSION: H120 x L120 x W45cm
MEDIUM: SENNA SIAMEA WOOD
COLOUR: YELLOW ORCHERE TO BURNT UMBER

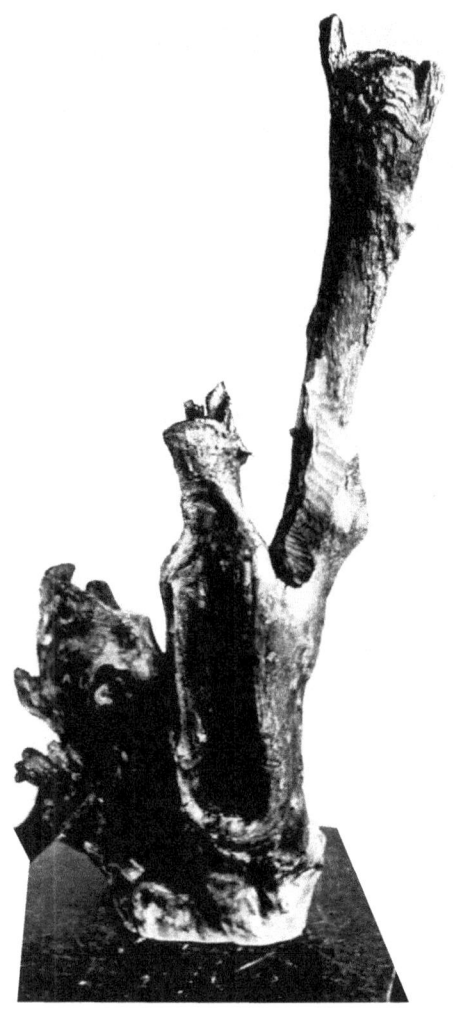

Ɔbragu in Akan literally means *Period of Despair*. Akan culture advocates the philosophy that Almighty God is the master provider. He is the provider of the needs of all creatures. Additionally, He is the father of all persons and as such manifests through his divine supremacy to satisfy the requests of His dependants. As the Creator of the universe nothing seems impossible for Him, therefore, with the Akan belief in the Almighty God as the provider of all things, African women must put their trust in Him for support in all ways.

This is a composition of a sitting mother breastfeeding her child. The composition is made from the lower portion of a tree trunk. It has some cracks and burns on the back of the mother and certain portions constituting the frontage. The mother's right arm is raised high with the palm and fingers forming a receptacle. The left arm runs towards the seat of the mother. Again, the palm and fingers are equally projected in a stretched out posture. This attempts to create despair. The lower limbs are covered with petal impression. The seat of the mother displays a portion of waist beads and part of the buttock. Invariably, the lower portion of the right foot appears in the left base of this composition.

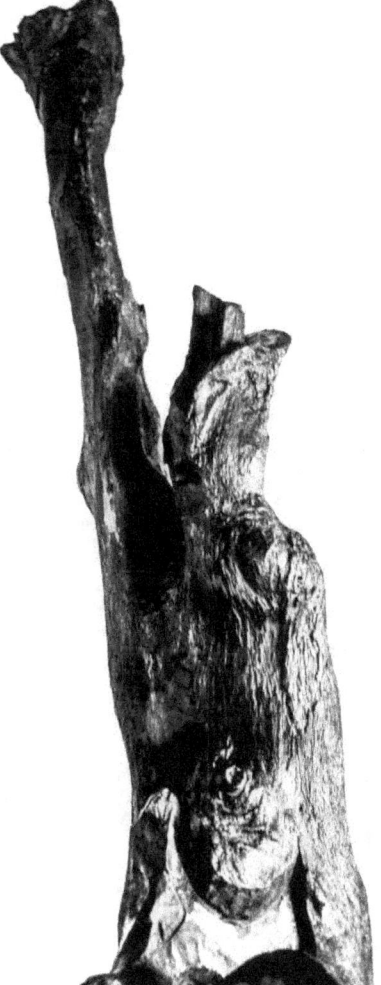

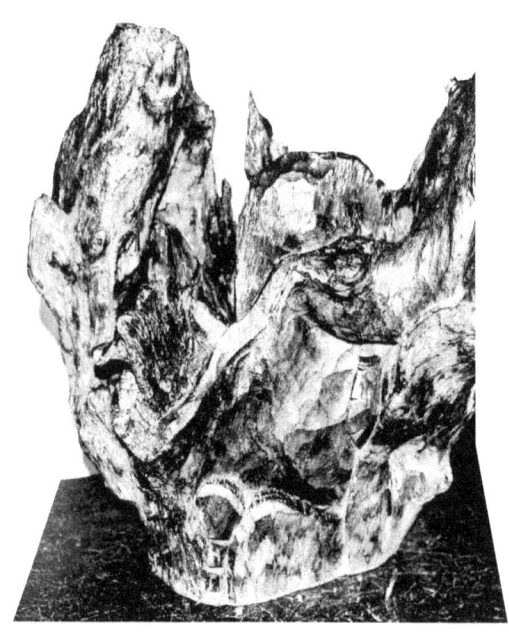

This composition replicates the form and pattern of the waist beads. The head of this mother which is stretched high up has no eyes and nose but rather a suggestive wide-opened mouth created from defective part of the top head. This defective portion also finds its trace at the back of the mother and this suggests the back of the body of the figure. The feeding child is carved out of the petal stalk of the composition. The child is seen connected to the vibrant and succulent breast of the mother rather than the other breast which is wrecked.

Ɔbragu symbolically represents the group of mothers who totally rely on the strength and support of the Creator at all times. The raised right arm of the figure with the receptacle palm reflects her willingness to accept all that are handed down to her by the Creator. This relationship with the Creator is cordial and reciprocal. She is ready to render the necessary appreciation to Him. The raised head and wide-opened mouth emphasize further the mother's relationship with the Creator, the Almighty God.

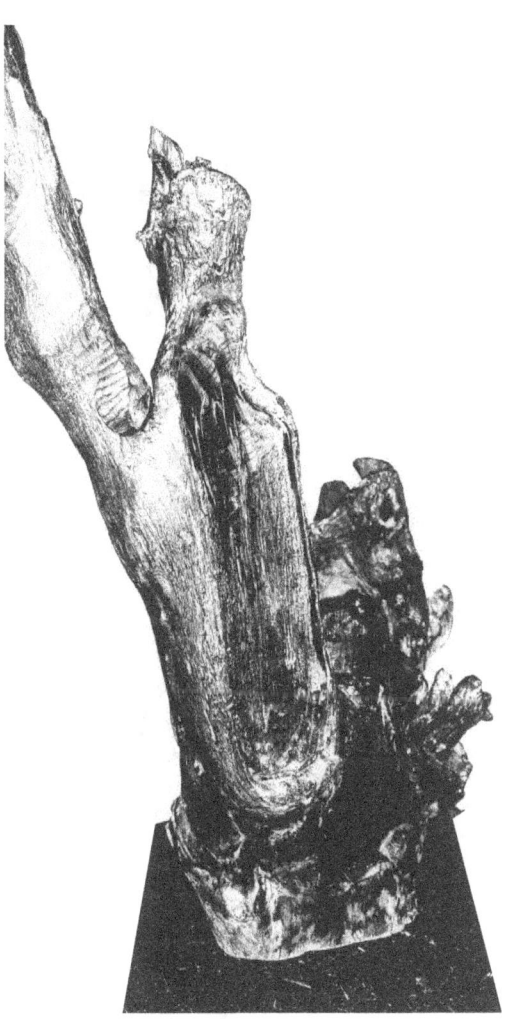

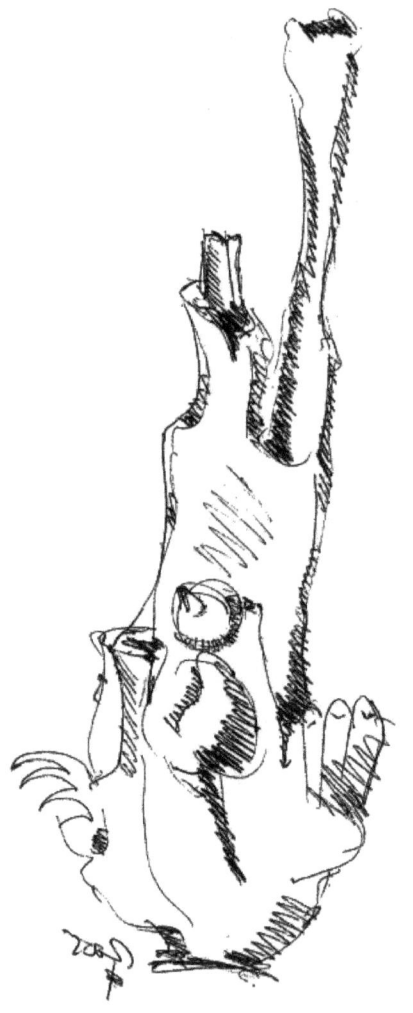

The petal or flowering impression over the lower portion of the figure signifies the hope that exists for all mothers whose bedrock is God. The cracked portion formed at the back of the mother, around the opened mouth of the mother and the portion of the lower base explains the long suffering and pain that afflict her in spite of the dependence and hope for better life.

Ɔbragu therefore presents to the African that in all situations and circumstances, there is always the need to depend on God, the Creator, rather than depend on minor mediums that may provide temporary solutions to human problems.

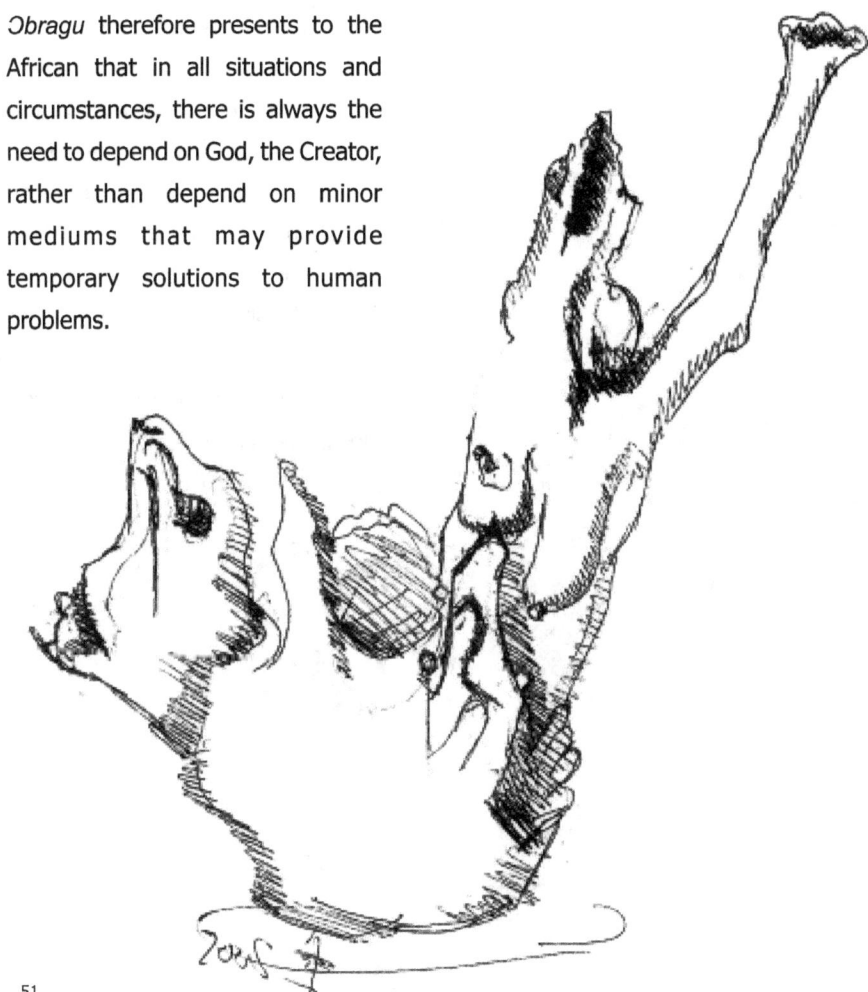

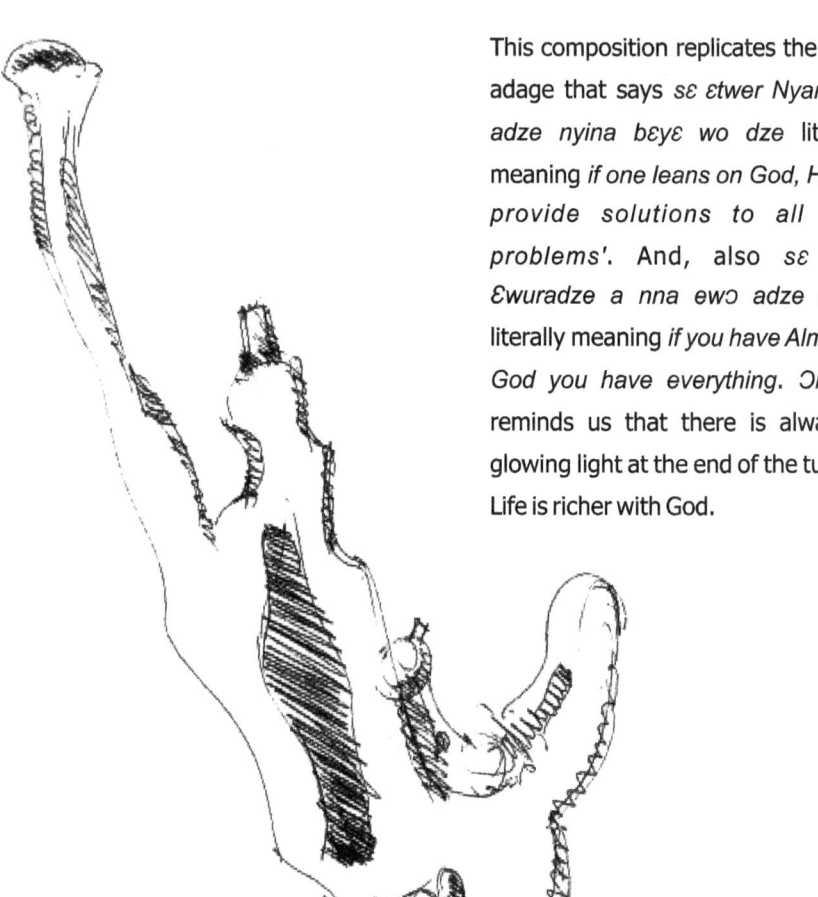

This composition replicates the Akan adage that says *sɛ ɛtwer Nyame a, adze nyina bɛyɛ wo dze* literally meaning *if one leans on God, He will provide solutions to all your problems'*. And, also *sɛ ɛwɔ Ɛwuradze a nna ewɔ adze nyina* literally meaning *if you have Almighty God you have everything*. Ɔbragu reminds us that there is always a glowing light at the end of the tunnel. Life is richer with God.

ƆYƐƐ MBA
(CREATOR OF CHILDREN)

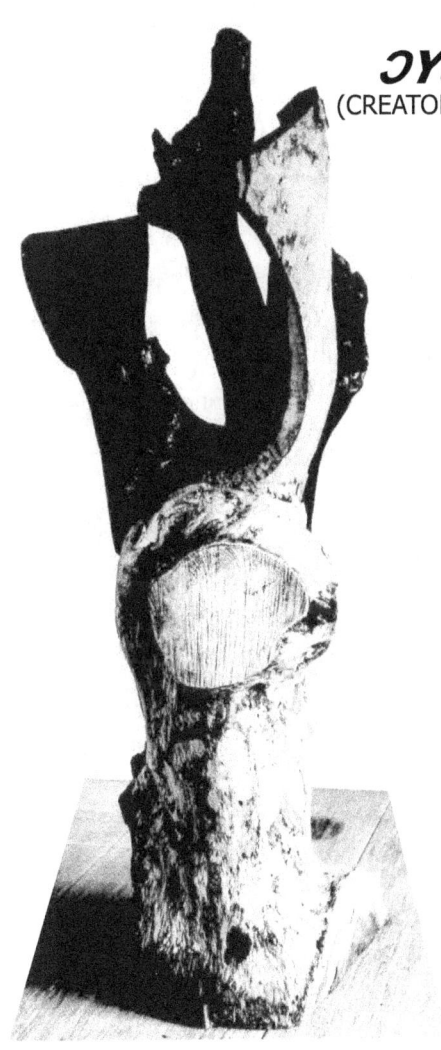

YEAR; 2005
DIMENSION: H75 x L60 x W60cm (EACH)
MEDIUM: SENNA SIAMEA WOOD
COLOUR: PALE YELLOW TO BURNT URMBER

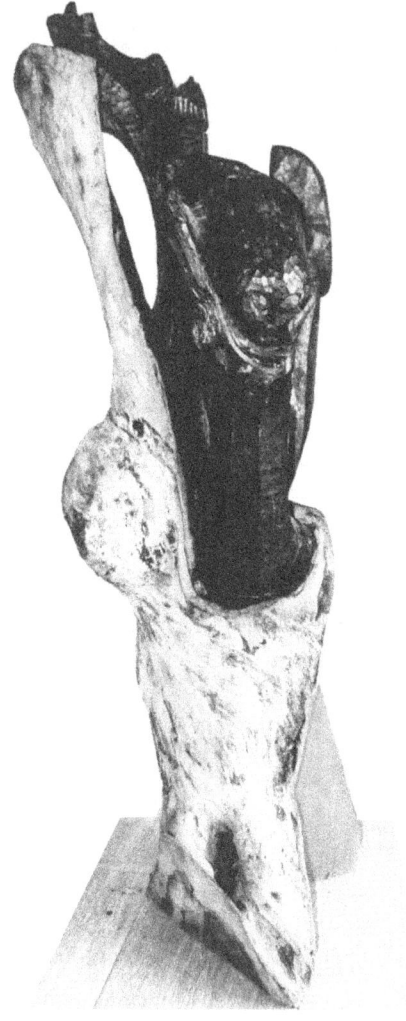

Ɔyɛɛ Mba in Akan literally means Creator of Children. Ɔyɛɛ mba is an Akan fertility deity. In the Akan culture, child bearing is the prime responsibility of women. Based on this belief, married women resort to all possible means to become fertile and fruitful in order to appease their loved ones, families and the community. Therefore, all married women who are not able to bear children may be regarded as sterile and suffering from a curse or a form of calamity.

Women who bear children are said to be enjoying the blessing of Almighty God, deities and ancestors. In the African culture, women are believed to be the providers of the blood that form children while fathers offer women and children the spiritual support. Traditionally, the role of Akan mothers is to replenish human stock and also serve as the channel through which ancestors return to the physical world.

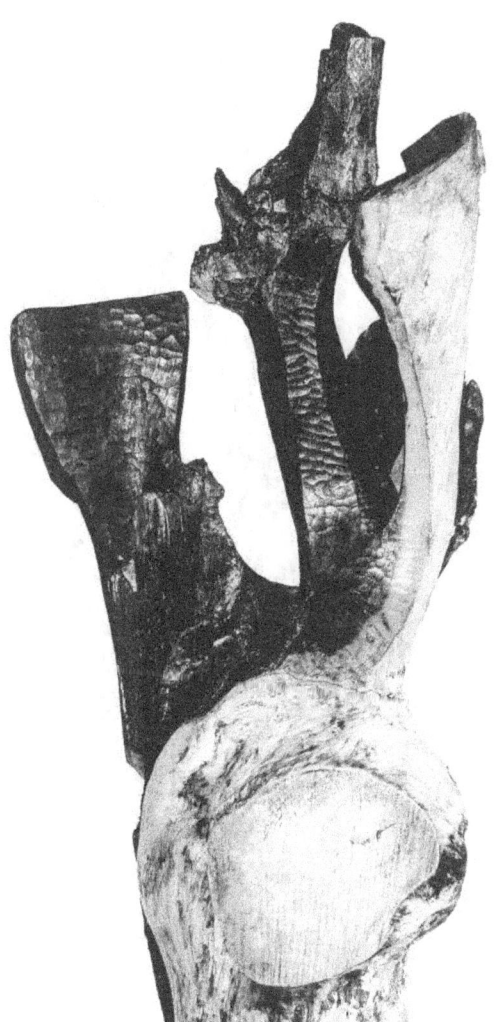

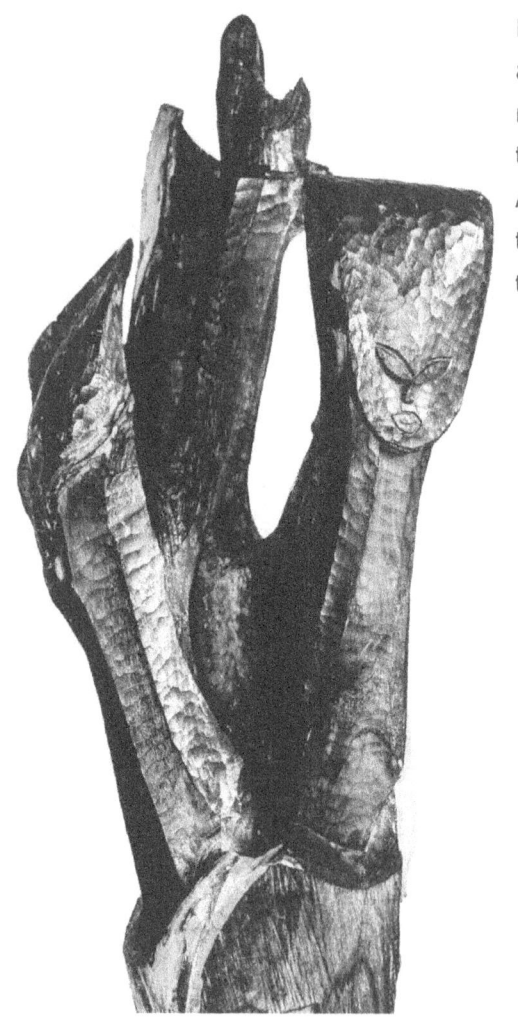

Hence, the fertility deity is always available to offer assistance to married women by interceding on their behalf and appealing to Almighty God, deities and ancestors to bless such needy women with their heart desired children.

Ɔyɛɛ mba is a composition of the mother bearing a set of twins. The first twin is positioned behind the mother as it is done by Akan mothers particularly when carrying their babies. The second twin is positioned at the side of the mother, a practice that has been in vogue among teenage mothers who perform portal duties. The faces of their children are turned away from their mothers' back. The mother's right upper arm holds the twin by the side while the left upper arm has been raised to the level of the long mouth. The head and face of the mother has been rendered in a long but slender model. The head of the children has a rendition of the Ekuaba (Doll) figure.

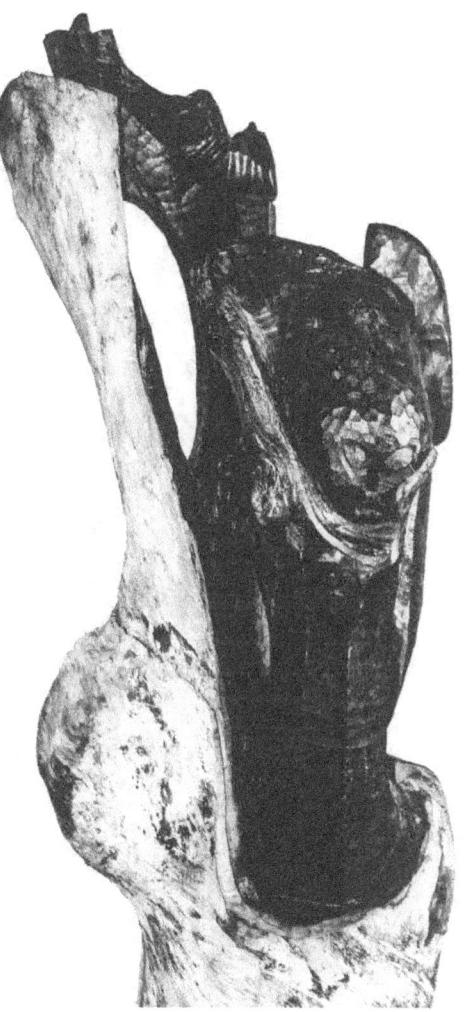

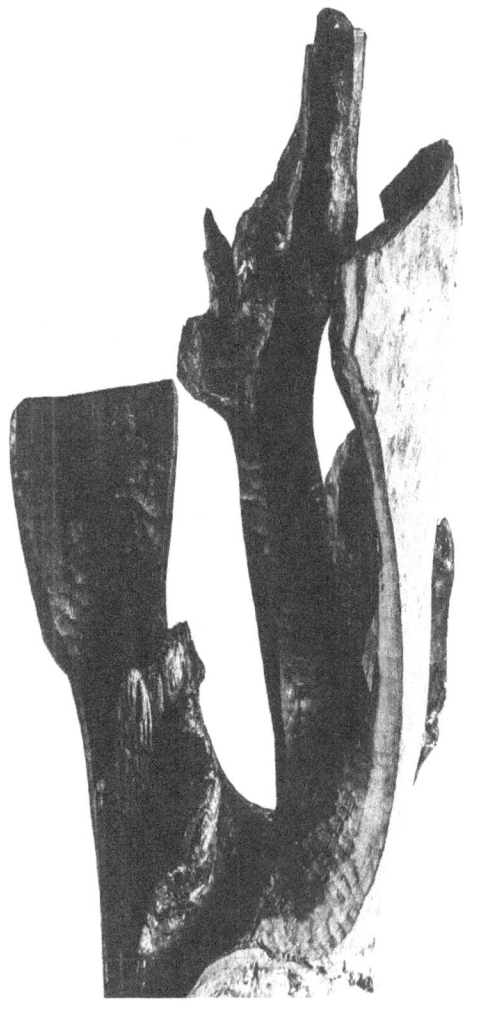

The composition projects a mother with juicy and bulky breasts in a cloth as it is usually done by Akan mothers to hold their breasts and cover their children concurrently. The juicy-bulky breasts are positioned using the natural tree bark. The lower part of the composition presents the uncarved portion of the tree (natural bark and sap of the tree). The back view of the composition presents a woven pattern resulting from the interlocking nature of the right arm, torso of mother and that of the twin held at the side of the mother.

Ɔyɛɛ mba is composed from a tree trunk that has three projections, an extension of the tree bark and a wedge base. Two of these projections constitute the twins that have disc heads. The third projection forms the head of the fertility deity. These are burnt umber in colour. The vertical extension of the tree bark has the inner colour as that of the three projections and the outer in a pale yellow colour just as the colour of the lower front part of the composition. The composition has a triangular wooden plank attached to the back of the wedge-like base which provides stability to the vertical sculpture piece.

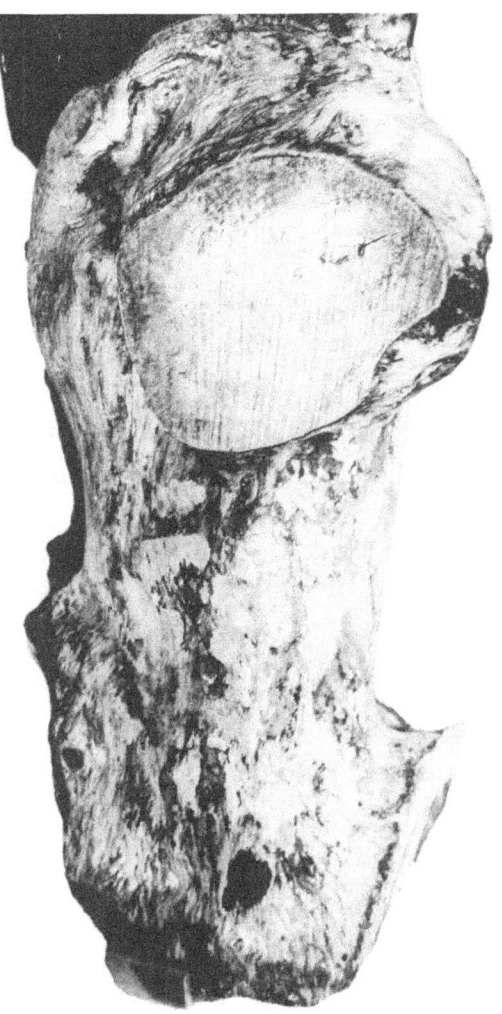

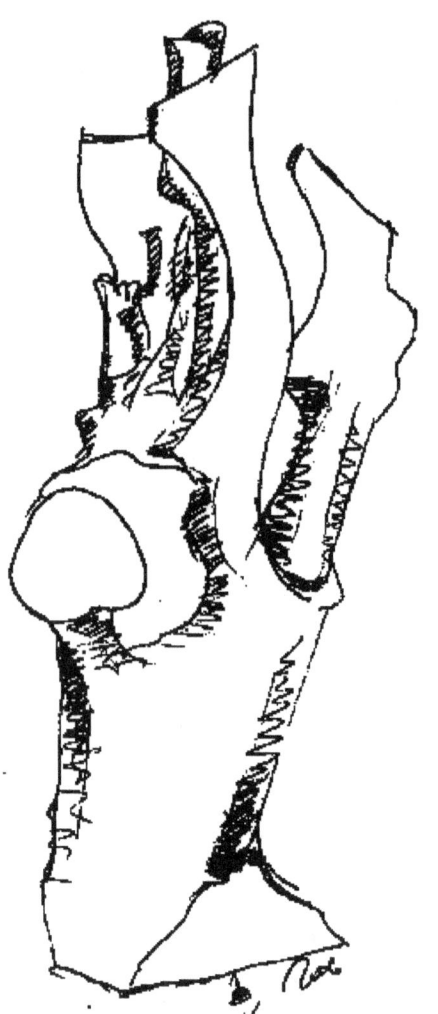

CONCEPT

Ɔyɛɛ mba projects the Akan female deity whose duty is to bless married women with children, protect women during pregnancy and also protect children from evil attacks, sickness and death. She is the symbol of life. The female figure is seen giving reverence to the ancestors, deities, praising and giving thanks to Almighty God for providing her with not one child but a set of twins. Africans believe that the process of reincarnation and rebirth only happens through women who are the vehicles upon which ancestors re-appear as human beings. Ɔyɛɛ mba possesses bulky and juicy breasts that are synonymous with African female sculptures and the philosophies of the breast of African women that are able to breast feed all children until they are weaned.

These provide children with the needed natural nutritional requirement for survival and physical growth. The composition projects a mother with bulky and juicy breasts in a wrapper cloth as done by Akan mothers to hold their breasts and cover their children concurrently. In communities where breasts are habitually exposed, insignificant sexual connotations are considered. Therefore, the bulky juicy breasts in the wrapper cloth, is synonymous with Akan married women who are sexually attractive to their male lovers for the purpose of procreation. The fully carved upper part of the figure that sits on the lower portion signifies how the needy and poor in the community are always relying on supernatural beings to provide them with their wants.

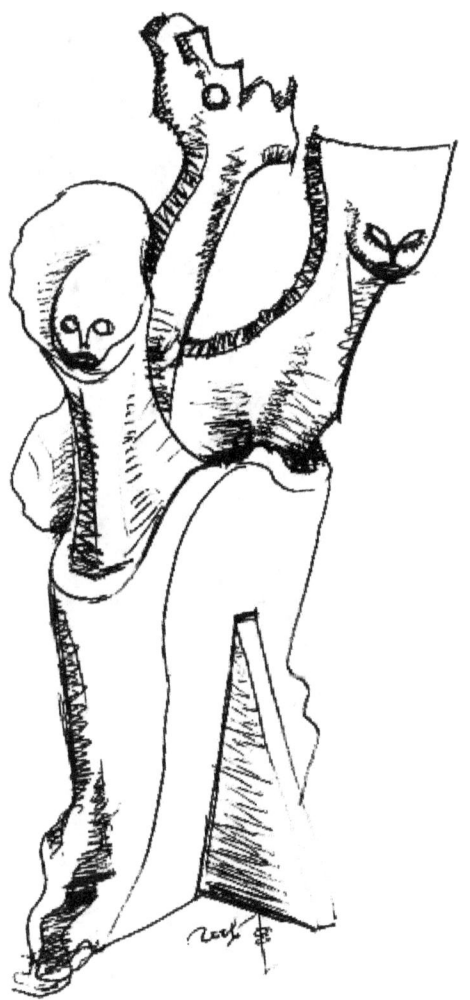

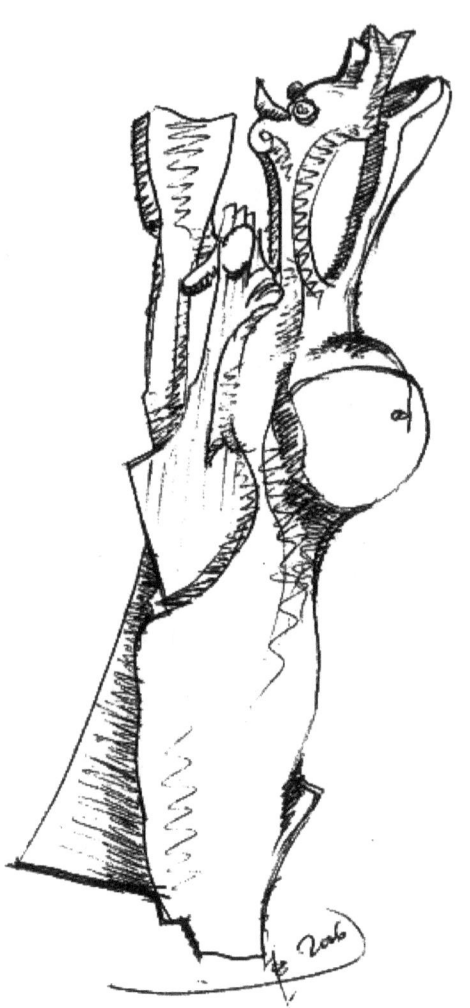

The natural tree bark and the sap of the tree represent all the Unseen spirits in the community who intervene, provide the needs and protect the vulnerable in the community. The back view of the composition presents a woven pattern emerging from an interlocking arrangement of the arm, the torso of mother and her twins. This shows the tension that results from a woman and her quest for a child. This wrestling situation appeals to the fertility deity to intervene for the Supreme Being to offer the necessary assistance and make the woman bear a child. The left upper arm raised high to the level of the mother's mouth, assumes the channel through which women transmit their plea and request. The long slender head and the face of the mother depict a sorrowful mood of the barren woman.

The *Ekuaba* head of the children expresses the love that Akan women have for children. It is drawn like the heart to symbolize love. The bulky and juicy breasts in the wrapper cloth signify the inextinguishable, nutritious and medicinal fluid that is always available and ready to feed and protect African children until they are weaned. *Ekuaba* is an Akan fertility doll that symbolizes fertility. It is also used formally and informally by infants and adolescents for recreation and motherhood training. *Ɔyɛɛ mba*, the provider of children, the Akan fertility deity, is always up to the task of providing married women with children, and ensuring their growth and protection against sickness and death.

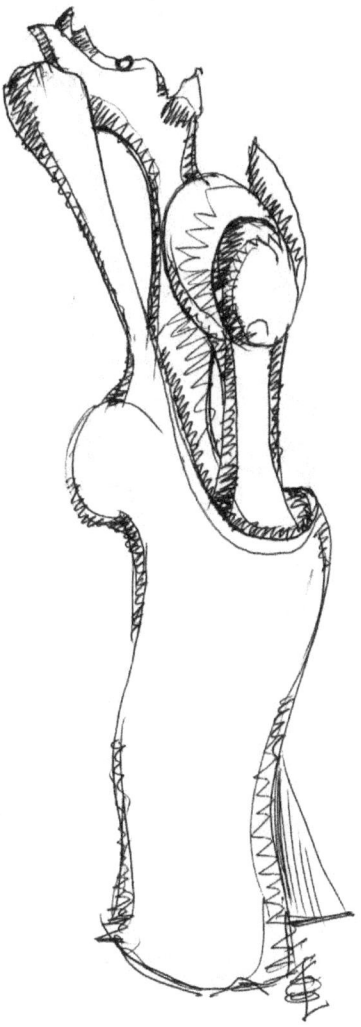

EGUDZE KORABAA
(FEMALE TREASURER)

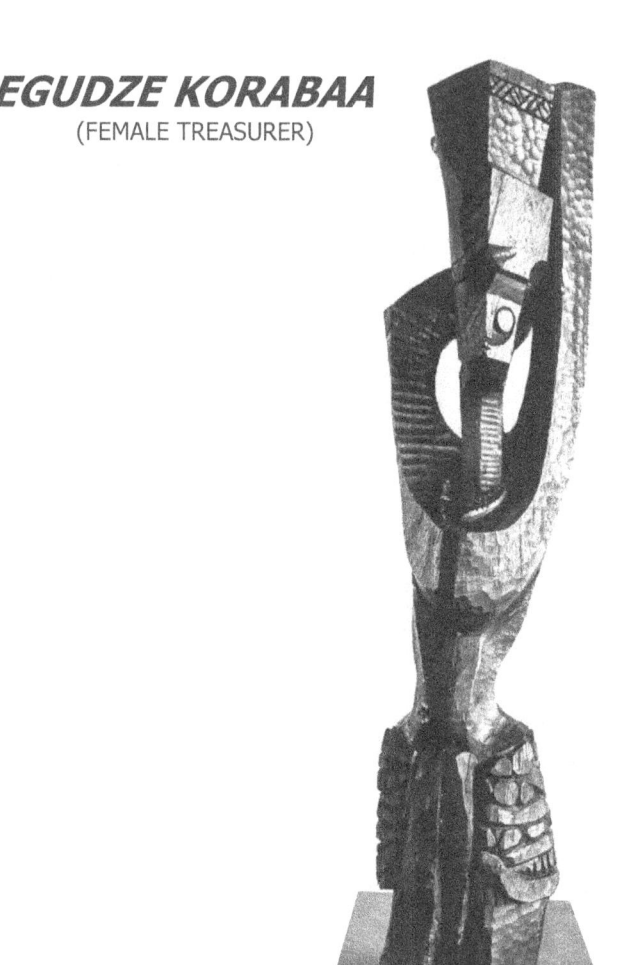

YEAR; 2003
DIMENSION: H110 x L30 x W25cm
MEDIUM: SENNA SIAMEA WOOD
COLOUR: PALE YELLOW AND BURNT UMBER.

Egudze Korabaa in Akan literally means *a Female Treasurer or Female Keeper of Treasury or Wealth*. The Akan culture presumes that females are the best preference to males in terms of keeping and maintaining treasure or wealth. Females are frugal and prudent in their spending. They are more cautious, practical, discreet and far-sighted when properties are entrusted to them. On the other hand, males are naturally more inclined to the dissipation of wealth or assets. They are reckless, hasty, frivolous, and light hearted and out of control when entrusted with property. This composition seeks to praise the female tactful nature at protecting and preserving assets.

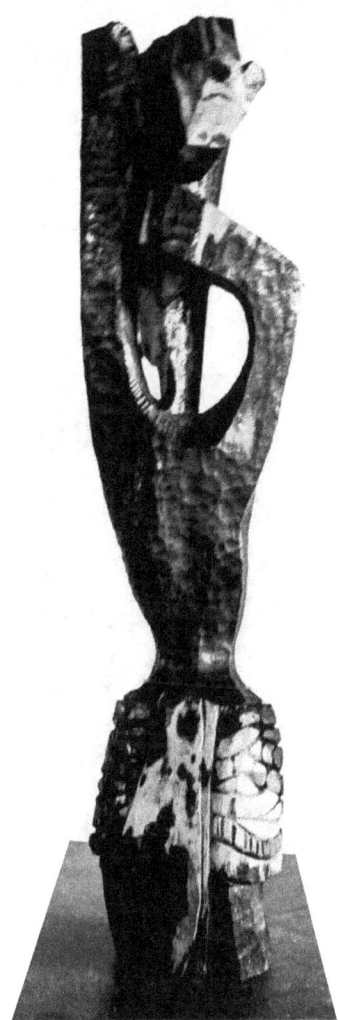

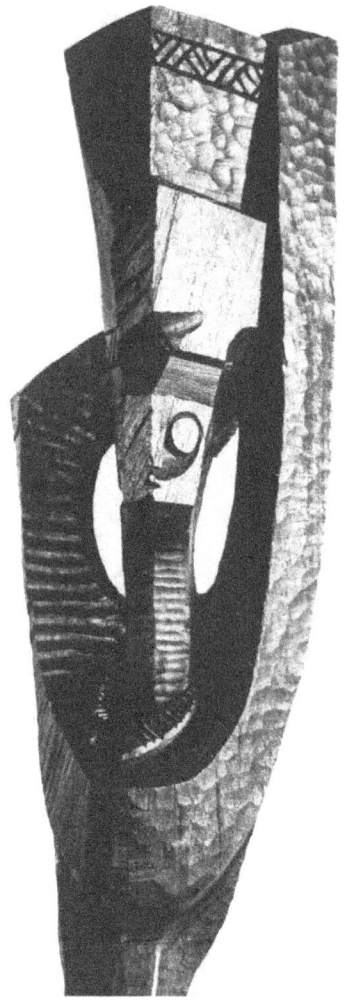

Egudze korabaa is a composition of a vertical posed female figure carrying a small container *(koraba)* and a torso. The composition is produced from a tree branch. The figure is dressed in traditional puberty apparel that comprises of a breast wrapper, an under-cloth and a set of indigenous Akan glass beads that run from the waist line through to the upper thigh, and also around the base of the neck.

She carries on her head a treasure pot *(Egudze koraba)*. The head of the figure is set in a forward looking posture. The female figure is not wearing any ornament on the ear. The left side of the face assumes a mask-like impression while the right side of the face shows chainsaw marks. The right portion of the treasure pot and the right side of the head reveal the harsh sun effects on the Senna Siamea tree.

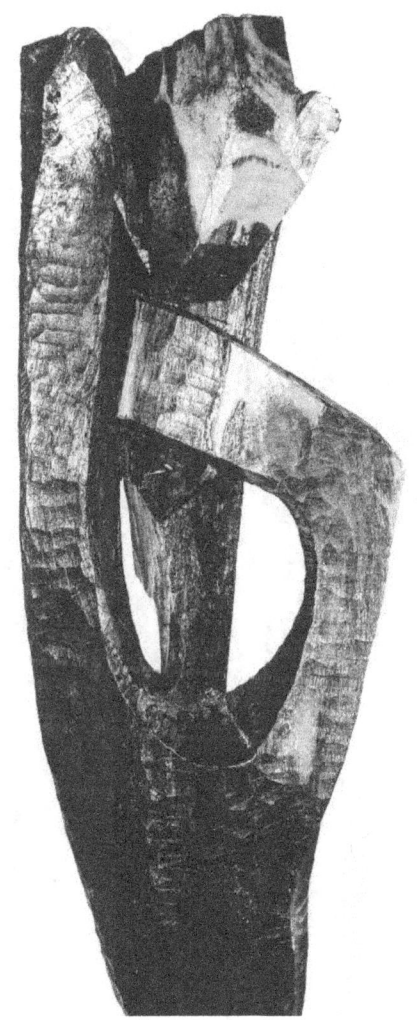

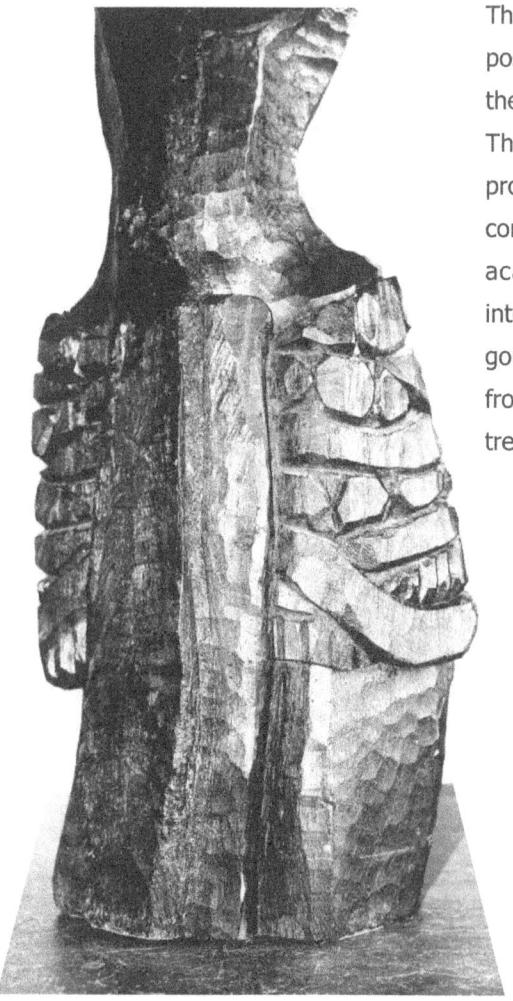

The upper arms of the figure are positioned at her back and across the front base of the treasure pot. These indicate an attempt to protect to the treasure. The entire composition, carved in the Western academicism style, shows an interaction with chainsaw marks, gouge patterns and smooth texture from the natural torch portion of the tree.

CONCEPT

Egudze korabaa is a presentation made to showcase the numerous benefits that abound in the culture of preservation and protection to the individual, family and community. Preservation of funds, physical properties, health, and ecology requires the effort of custodians and trustees to provide security and protection. Assets acquired and bequeathed need protection from adversaries and squanderers. Therefore, the trustees and custodians are required to ensure proper management and accountability.

In the composition, a treasure pot *(Egudze koraba)* is being carried on the head of a female youth in a ceremonial apparel which symbolizes puberty, innocence and clean spirit of an indigene required in the preservation of the individual, family and community assets.

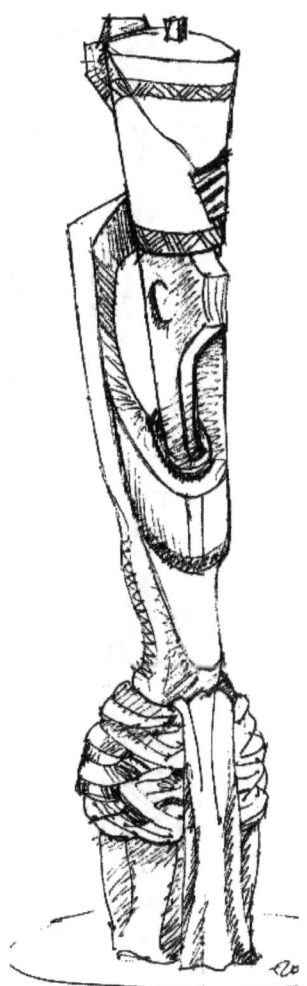

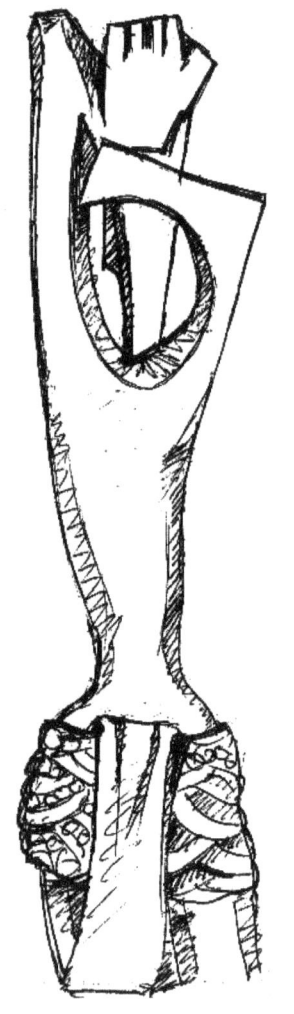

The position of the upper arms and hands behind and around the base of the treasure pot, *(Egudze koraba)*, signifies the effort by all and sundry to provide some protection for the assets and wealth owned by people and the community since dissipation of wealth is commonplace. However, saving money and preserving properties are not given enough attention by the community. Non-saving and preservation are seen to be undesirable to the community members. Females are presumed to be more transparent and more prone to accountability. Women culturally tend to hold, preserve and protect assets and wealth.

Upper arms of the figure are positioned at her back and across the front base of the treasure pot, breast wrapper, an under-cloth are evident of the preservative and protective culture of women. The adage *mbaa na wɔ dze egudze sie yie* literally implying in Akan that *women are the best preservers and protectors of family assets and wealth*. The indigenous Akan glass beads running from the waist line provides support and protection to the under-cloth which also in turn offers protection to the vitality of the woman. Hence, the composition *Egudze korabaa* validates the foregoing concept of treasure keeping by females.

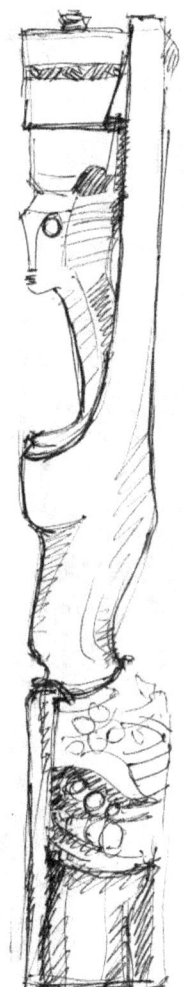

ENA NO DƆ
(MOTHER'S LOVE)

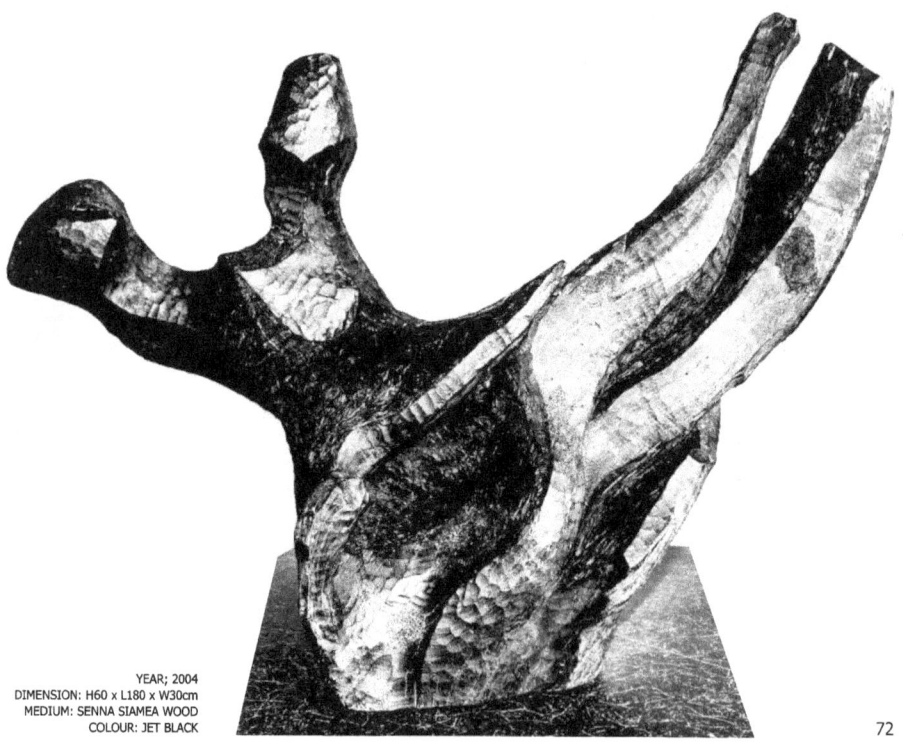

YEAR; 2004
DIMENSION: H60 x L180 x W30cm
MEDIUM: SENNA SIAMEA WOOD
COLOUR: JET BLACK

Ena No Dɔ, in Akan literally means *mother's love*. In Akan culture, mothers are believed to be the providers of the blood that formed their children while fathers offer them their spirit. Traditionally, the role of Akan mothers is to raise children especially at home. This includes bathing, feeding, laying the baby to sleep and forming the language base of the child among others. This allows children to spend more time with the mothers while their fathers are almost absent in their homes in search of treasure. In addition, since Akans are matrilineal in inheritance automatically children will tow their mothers' line. Hence, the Akan adage *akokɔba nndzii akokɔ nyin ekyir* literally meaning, *a chicken never follows a cock*.

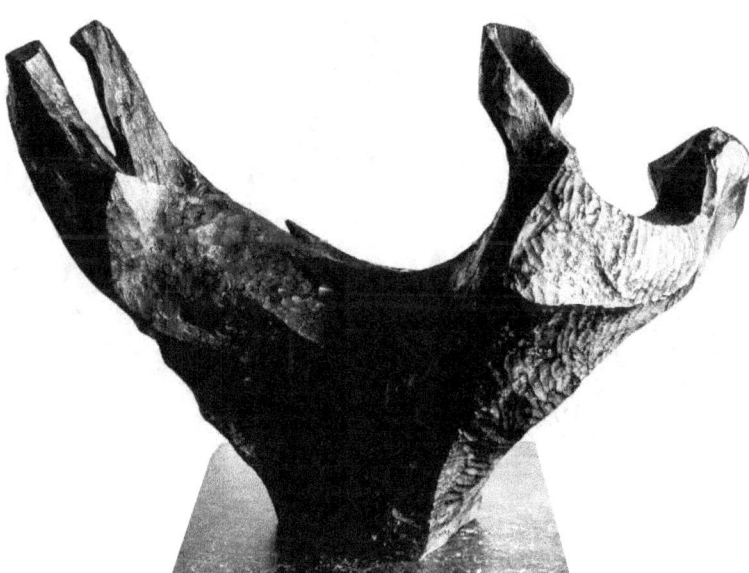

Ena no dɔ is a composition of a mother and child in romance. The mother is set in a reclining pose and has her legs raised high into a diagonal position. The head of the child which is the only displayed part of the body is held high up. The mother torso and that of the body of the child are all wrapped in a cloth that drips onto the base of the composition. The head of the mother and that of the child are cast in a cordial relationship. *Ena no dɔ* exhibits the steadfast love that exists between mother and child, community and indigenes, superior and subordinate, etc.

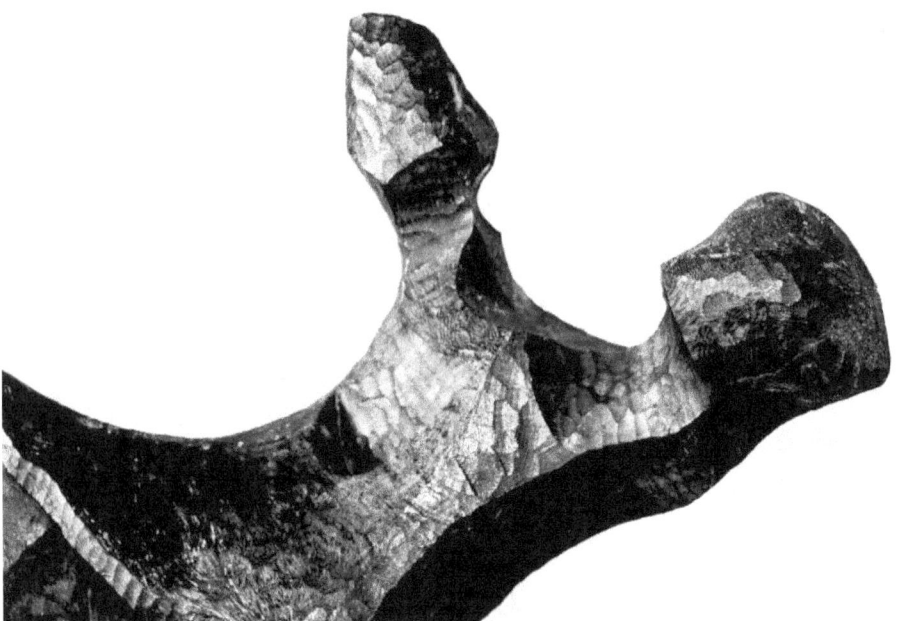

CONCEPT

Ena no dɔ symbolizes the unflinching love a mother has for her child and vice versa. The mother represents the community and the child stands for the indigenes or the community members. The mother demands from her child deep love, care, support, dedication, concern, and respect. Persons who are in love ensure that they provide and accord their loved ones the attributes of love. They equally demand of their lovers the same attributes- care, respect, support, honour, etc.

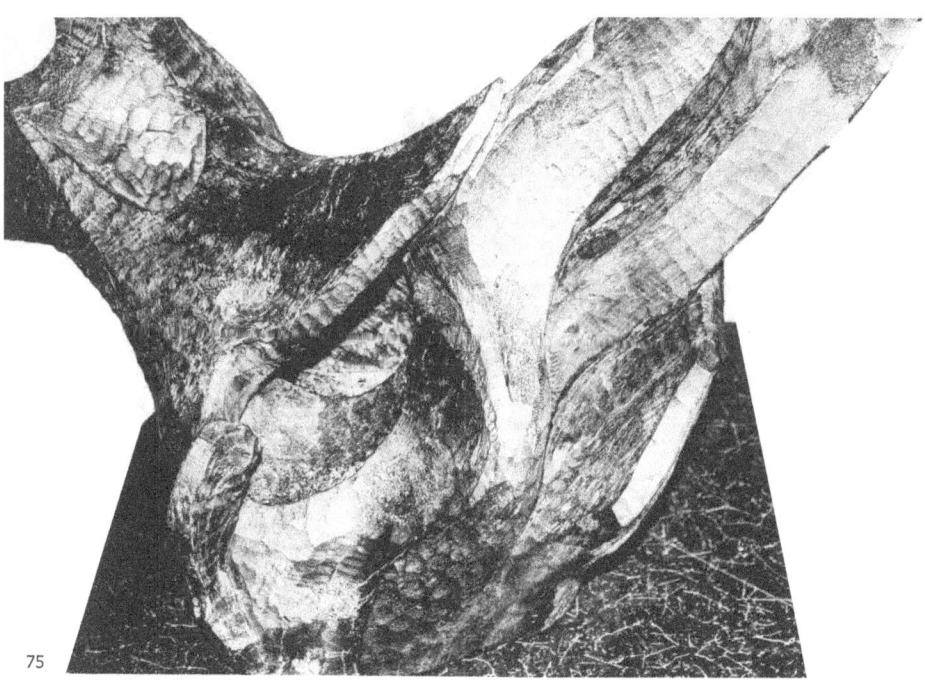

Like a mother's love toward a child, the community leaders are expected to offer their indigenes security, social and economic empowerment, hope and better life. The indigenes are equally required to pledge their allegiance, support, commitment, and loyalty for community leaders. This reciprocity of love ensures peaceful co-existence, social and economic growth, spiritual and physical upliftment progress and development in the community. This also ensures the continuity of the community's life cycle. Love for one's nation, love for one neighbour and love for oneself will promote the very essentials of life that lead to human fulfilment.

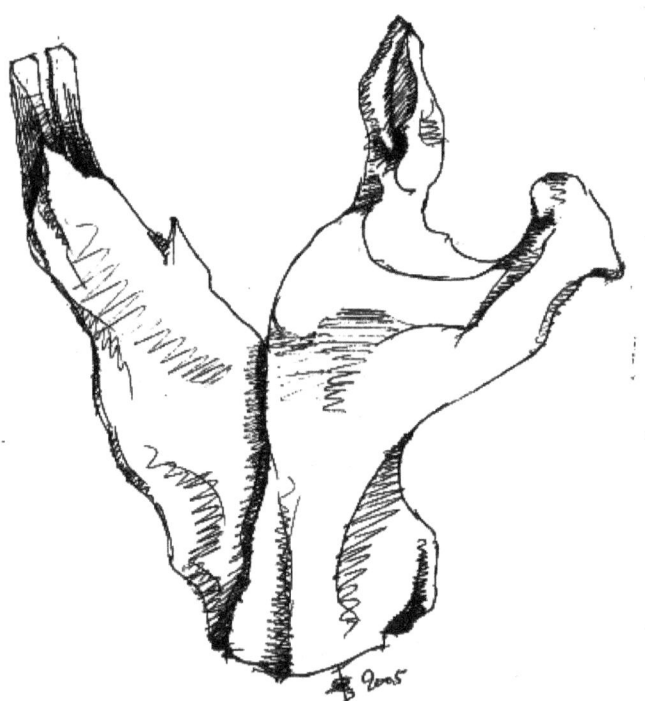

The projected head of the mother and that of the child connote a linkage that exists between a community and its indigenes. It is supposed to be cordial, smooth, and direct. The wrapped cloth over the mother's torso and the body of the child portrays the extent to which their nudity could be shared. This promotes unrestricted contact between the community and its indigenes thereby reassuring transparency, integrity and honesty in the management of the community's wealth. The raised legs of the mother into the diagonal direction offer the community the hope for a better future.

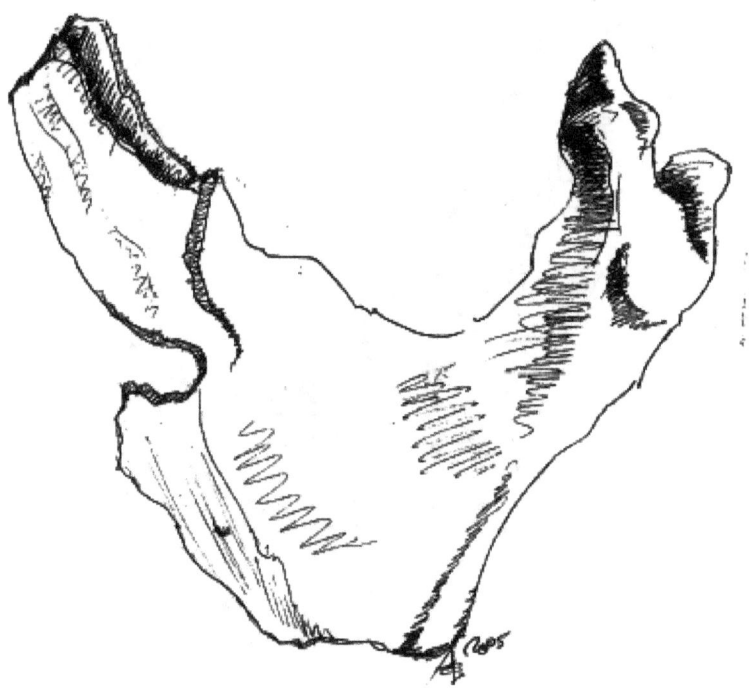

The uniform colouration of the Senna Siamea wood presents to the community a natural harmony and ambience that exist within a progressive and prosperous environment. There is an Akan adage that says that *Obaatan na onyim dza ne mba bedzi* and also *abofra a ɔhwe ne na no, ɔtaa nyin kyɛr* literally meaning *only mothers know what is best and proper for their ward and children*. It is believed that the elderly will live longer if this provision is made. It could be said that, the closeness of the physical and spiritual bond of the mother and child pervades their soul and being and propels them to greater heights for prosperity and progress.

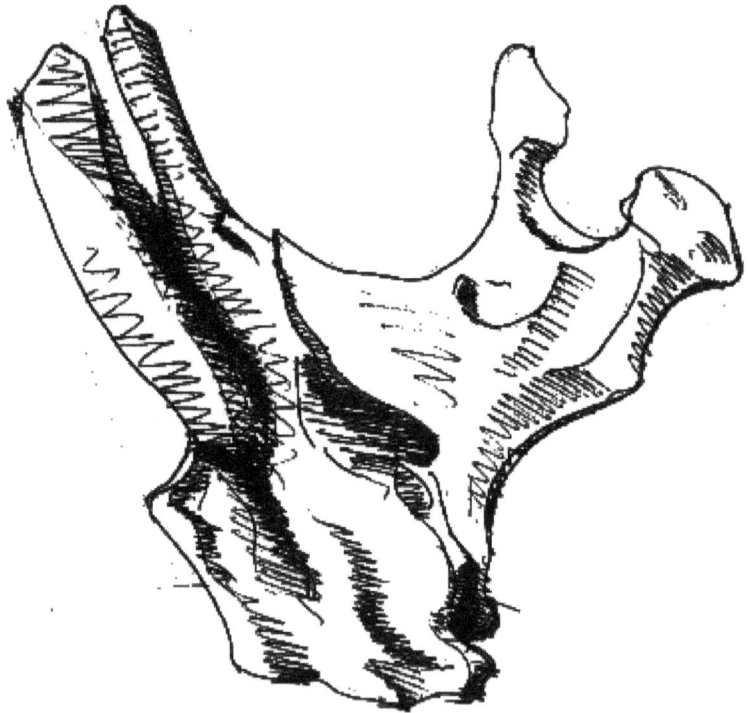

ITU A ENNKƆPEM
(FLIGHT TO SAFETY)

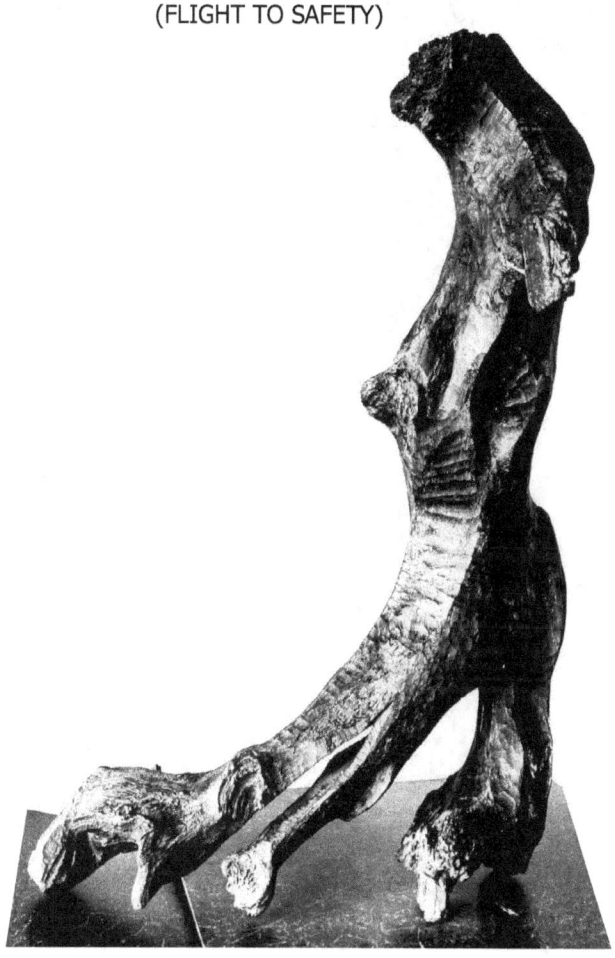

YEAR; 2004
DIMENSION: H90 x L90 x W50cm
MEDIUM: SENNA SIAMEA WOOD
COLOUR: JET BLACK

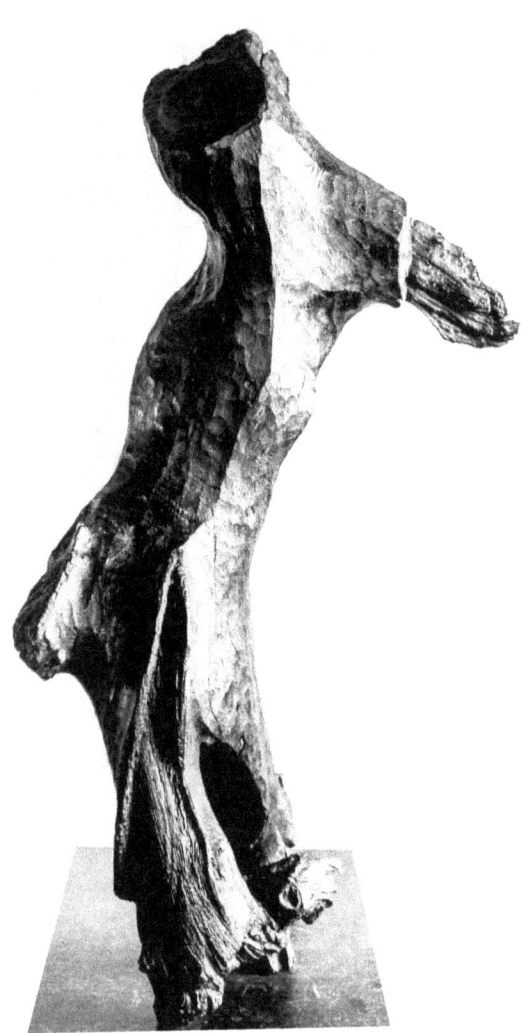

Itu A Ennkɔpem in Akan literally means *Flight to Safety*. Among the Akans, success is a divine gift handed down to them by Almighty God. The general belief is that the Akans are naturally endowed with certain talents, skills and trade that make them wealthy above other ethnic groups. Additionally, in Ghana, most all the nation's natural resources reside in the Akan localities. It is therefore not surprising that Akans are very confident. They have the strength of character, pride, expensive life-style and are successful. The African community encourages the acquisition of wealth through genuine and practicable means.

80

This composition is made from a tree trunk that is attached to its roots. It depicts a youthful male in a swift movement. The figure is in a top shift pose and its lower portion stretches backwards. It has an inclined top right arm with the hand attached to the body but stretched ahead of the figure. This arm has the elbow appearing further behind the torso. The left upper arm appears short and has been stretched to the left direction almost horizontal towards the back. The hand, elbow and hair of the figure expose some degree of burnt and harsh sun rays effects on them. The figure has a recessed face with an indication of the mouth culminating from a defect on this portion of the tree.

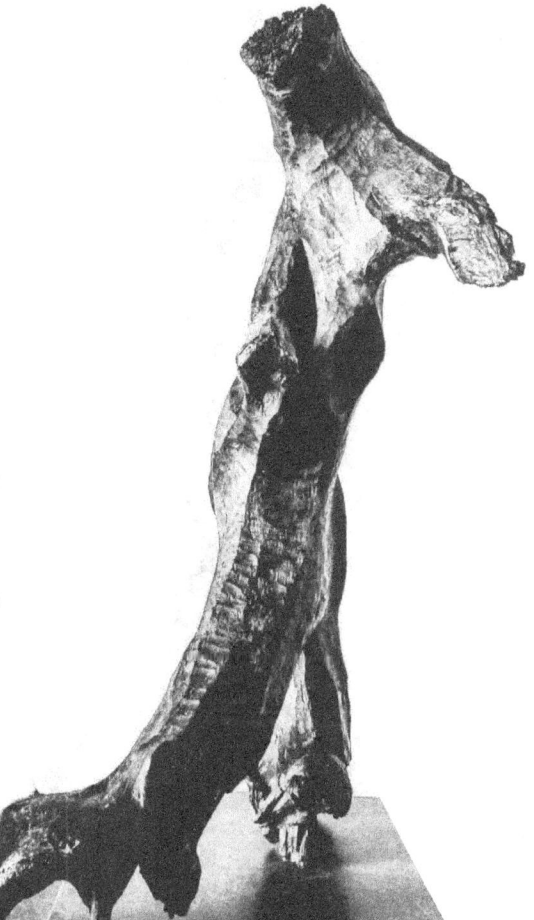

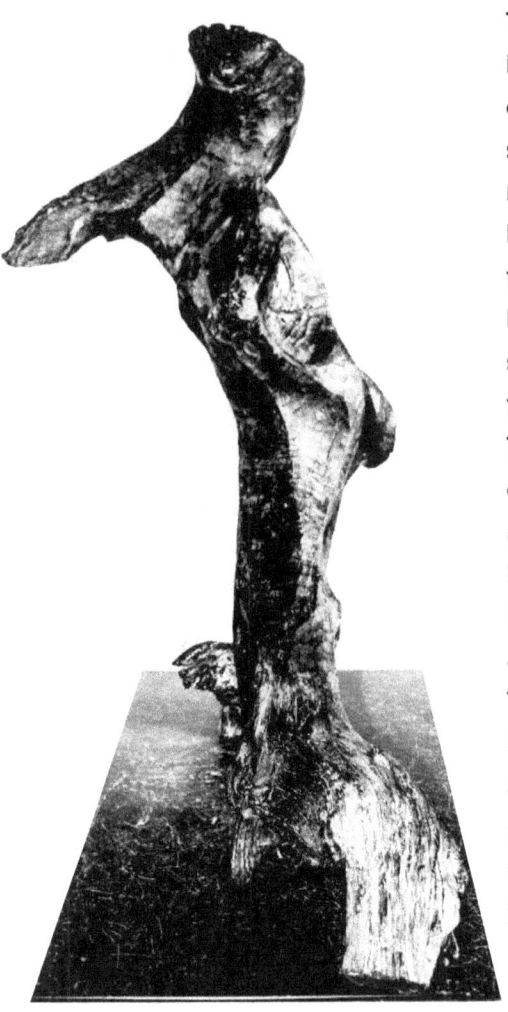

The lower limbs express an impression of the tree's roots. These exhibit several surface cracks, end-splits, knots and burns. The vertical root represents the right leg that has been set forward to assume a forward stepping posture. At the lower base of this leg, there are several knots that present the toes that are set in a reverse direction. The left leg that stretches backward, expresses a sprung posture that results from the previous step. This leg has a bulky foot and an end-split part representing some piled energy and tension from a previous stem. This posture suggests a swift movement of a figure in an aerodynamic and drag posture; a posture that is capable of flying to success irrespective of all opposing forces.

CONCEPT

Itu a ennkɔpem expresses the readiness of the African youth to step forward, strive hard, persevere, and forge through all the odds to achieve excellence. The composition seeks to encourage the African youth to resist all social, political, economic, educational and cultural barriers that impede human progress. These youth must acquire the necessary skills and knowledge that are required to propel the individual into prosperity. Like the Akan adage *sɛebɔ wokar a nna wosoa wo adze* which literally means *if you make an effort then a helper will be there to offer you the necessary assistance.*

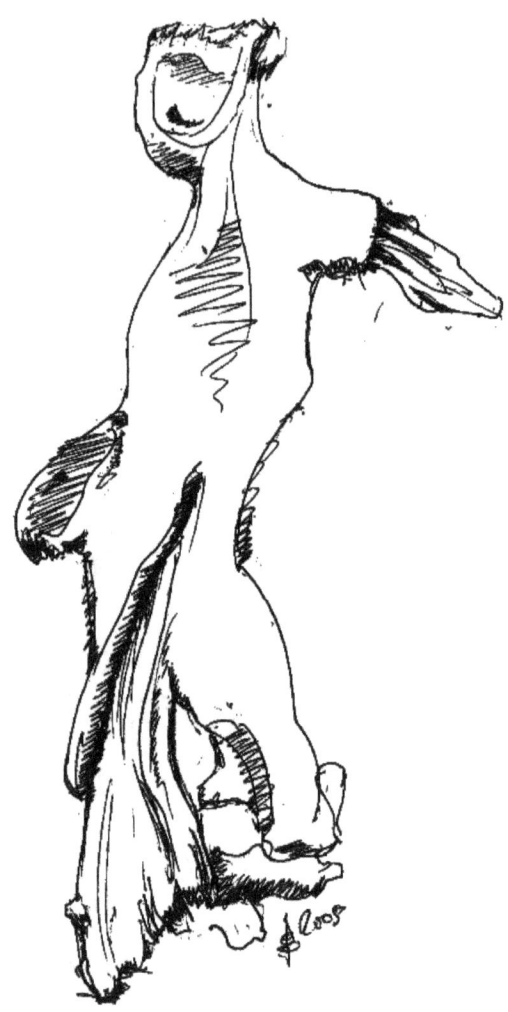

The African environment may be hostile, limited or challenging; there is the need for one to bolster courage and the preparedness to delve into greater heights of endeavour in order to achieve the best. The African youth need to stretch their thoughts; dream big, practicalise the dream, but make a modest start. Even though, there may be obstacles in one's life there is the need for one to be mentally upright and strong in thought in order to achieve the set goals. As said in Ghanaian parlance, 'one needs to be bold, strong and focused to achieve his own God given glory and destiny.

84

The dream must be big to start with and should not be dropped in the face of the challenges that may emerge. This dream can be definitely achieved. In realistic terms, one may not be fairly educated, be an alumni of a prestigious college or school, born to riches, possess an esteemed family name, be physically challenged or socially downgraded, you still require an inner spirited effort necessary to make a considerable progress in one's life. Hence, one should bold, strong and focused.

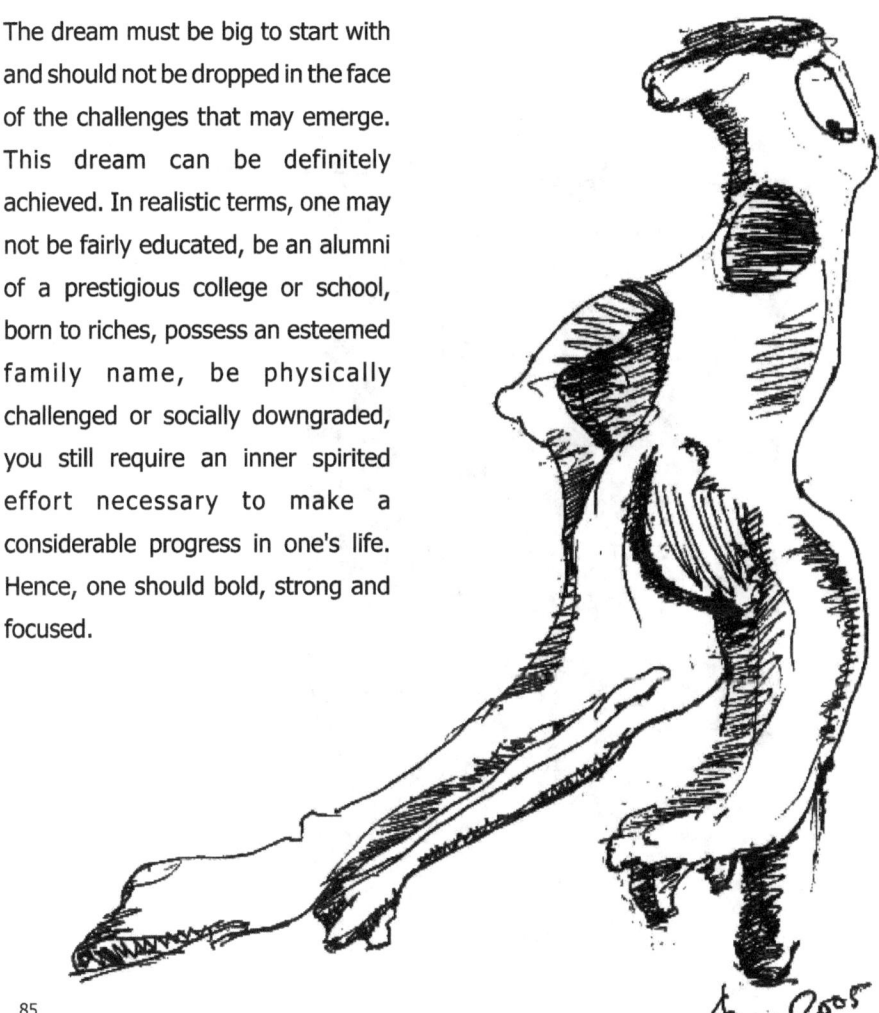

FAHODZI
(FOREVER FREE)

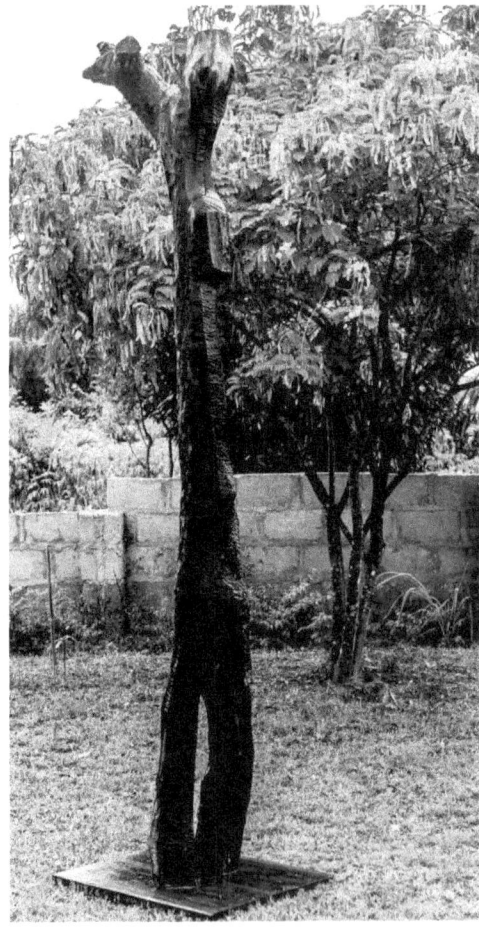

YEAR; 2005
DIMENSION: H300 x L75 x W50cm
MEDIUM: SENNA SIAMEA WOOD
COLOUR: OFF WHITE AND BLACK

86

Fahodzi in Akan literally means *Forever Free* or *Freedom*. In the Akan culture, hard work is rewarded with success. A person who endures the pain of work and is able to do so relentlessly will eventually break off the shackles that surround economic, social and political demands of an individual or community. The African believes in the dignity of labour, hence the adage *nsa a ɔnnyɛ edwuma no, onndzidzi,* meaning *lazy hands go hungry.*

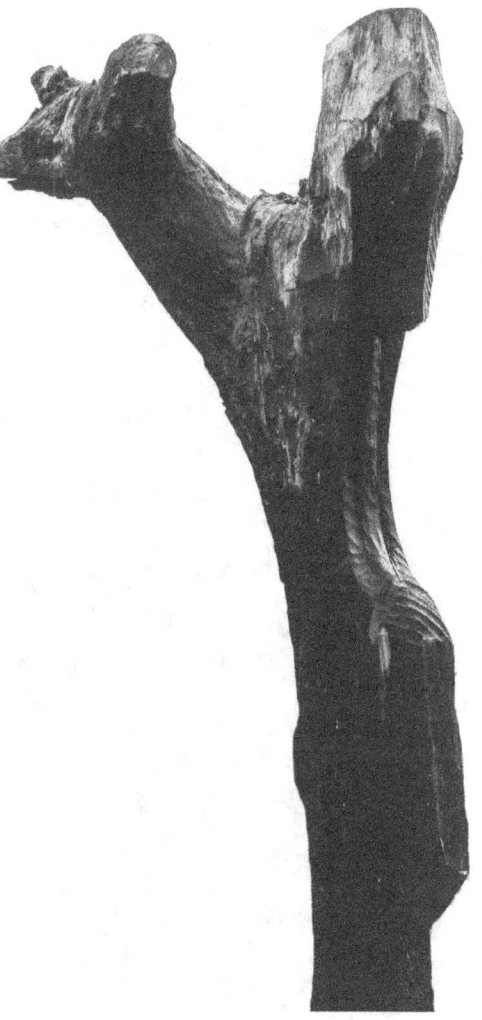

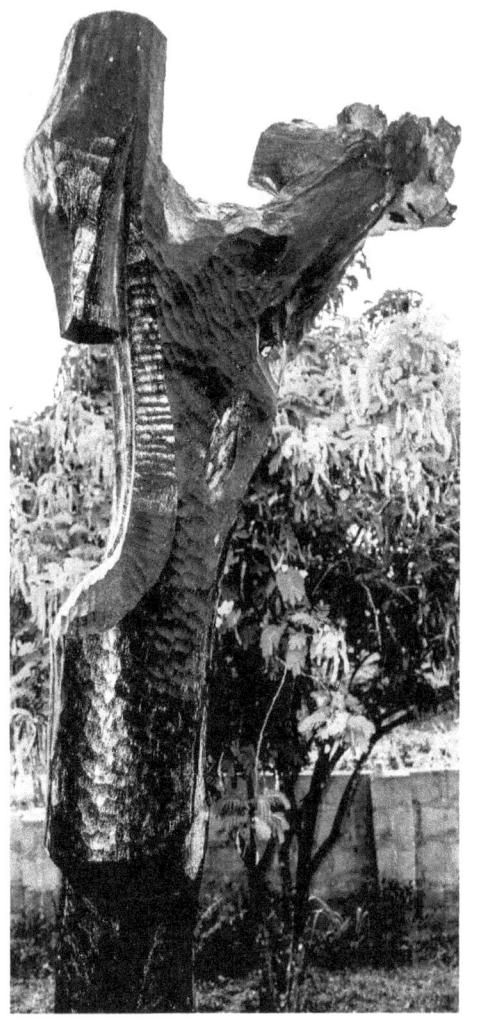

Fahodzi, a pole-sculpture, is a composition of a female figure posed in an out-stretched standing posture. The figure is composed from a pole tree trunk that has an off shoot at the top and a parted lower portion stuck into a rectangular wooden board. This provides some form of stability to the vertical sculpture piece. This is a frontal posed figure that has the neck stretched forward and the upper arms stretched backward. Her legs are parted at the lower portion. The composition has very little carved portion with a natural treatment and traces of destruction on it.

The figure has an elongated torso that bears the bulging breast and slightly protruded stomach. The outstretched hands of the figure bear the natural off-shoot or branch of the tree trunk. No human effort was put into this portion. The face has been fully carved leaving the two natural dentations that represent the eyes. The face has been carved into a narrow African mask that represents a goat's face. The wedge-like neck that holds the head slots into the top part of the chest up and above the breast. The bulging breast and the elongated torso have been presented with a well arranged tactile gouge finish. This finishing extends to the lower portion or the legs.

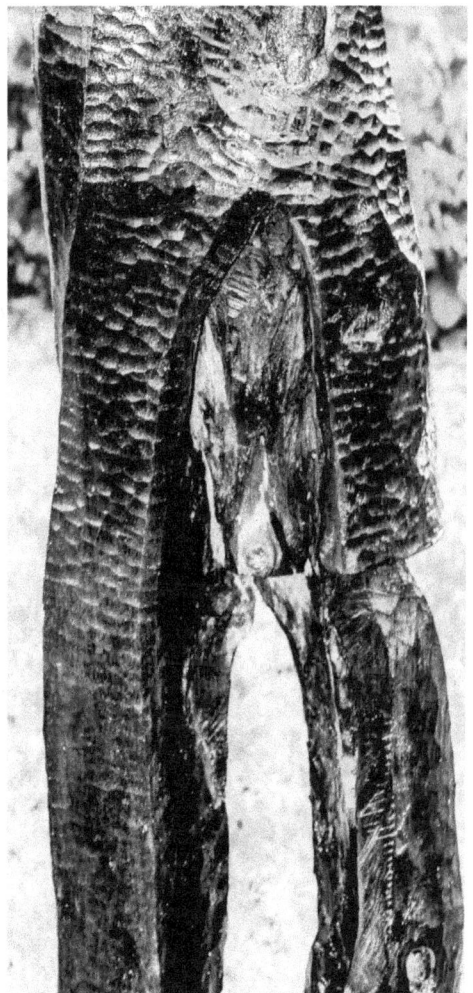

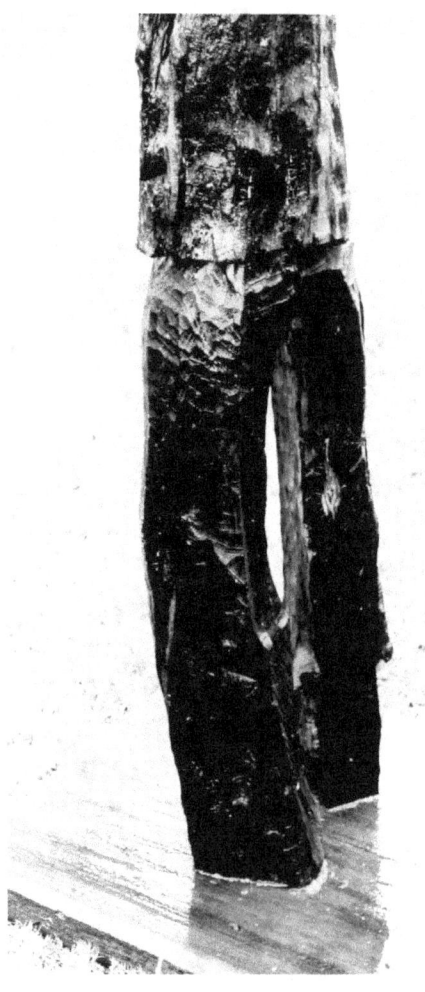

The natural texture of the burnt tree, insect attack and traces of rot are kept untouched. These stretch from the top right to the right bottom and the entire back of the figure. The fire and insect attacks cover the area in between the legs and the external part of the right leg. Traces of the black patches constitute the scorched effect on the face and part of the apparel. The torso has both the natural and artificial tactile finish that intersperse perfectly with burns, pin holes, and crack lines. This surface treatment that runs through the composition brings out its naturalness. The figure is dressed in the traditional African casual attire comprising of a light head gear that drips down the right side of the neck and the cover-cloth tied around the chest. The torso has been swung from right to left. This part has also received a plainal and geometric rendition. The same applies to the neck.

CONCEPT

Fahodzi is a composition that rewards hard work with success. The pole figure stretches to break off the shackles that surround economic, social and political demands of an individual or a community. The natural agents of destruction – bush fire, thunder, lightning, storms and rains attack the timber and create situations such as poverty, loss of relations etc. Socially, all humans are expected to withstand the vagaries of life. Insect attacks found on the composition reflect the extent to which the social fabric of the community has been affected. These, if not curbed, will definitely cause destruction to the progress of man.

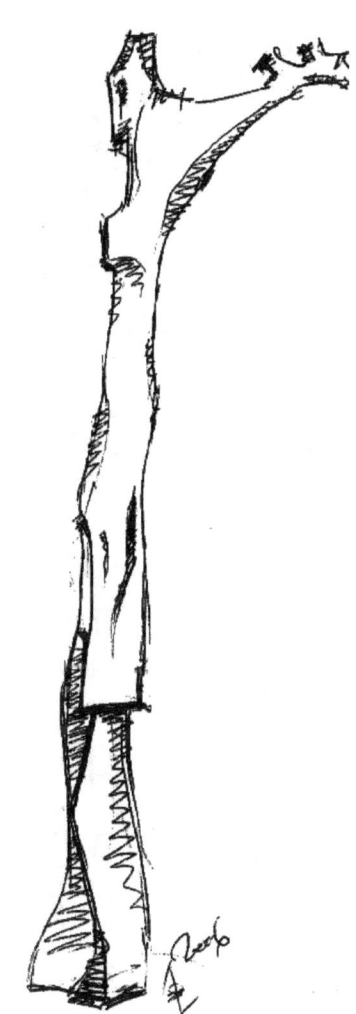

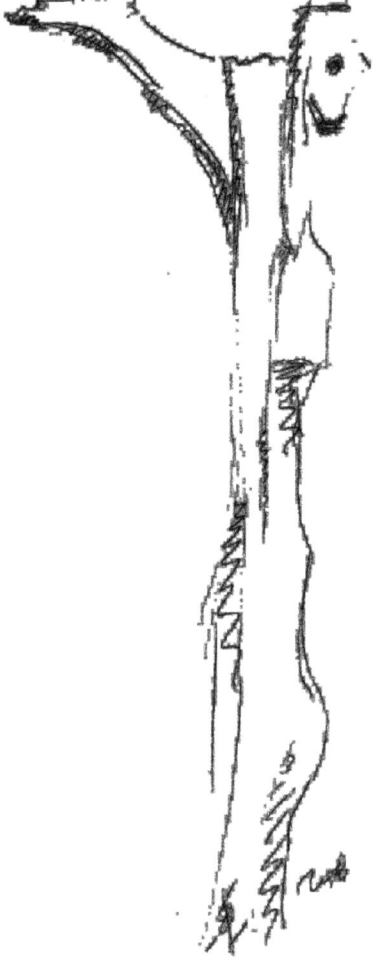

Symbolically, social, economic and political policies propounded by educational, political, social, family leaders and their like live to mete out harsh measures that go to thwart the efforts of individuals and communities. The goat face represents one's resilience to surmount any unbearable pressure that emerges from social disorders and economic breakdown and ability to make impact on the lives of others.

Fahodzi expresses the essence of hard work over economic, social and political pressures. Like the Bible parlance, once free, forever free. Individuals who are naturally able to work extra hard are able to make economic gains. This helps them overcome their social demands and better their political positions in the family and community. More so, persons who are economically stable are socially accepted by their own people. There is an Akan adage that says *edwumadzen ma nkonyimdzi* literally meaning *hard work rewards success*.

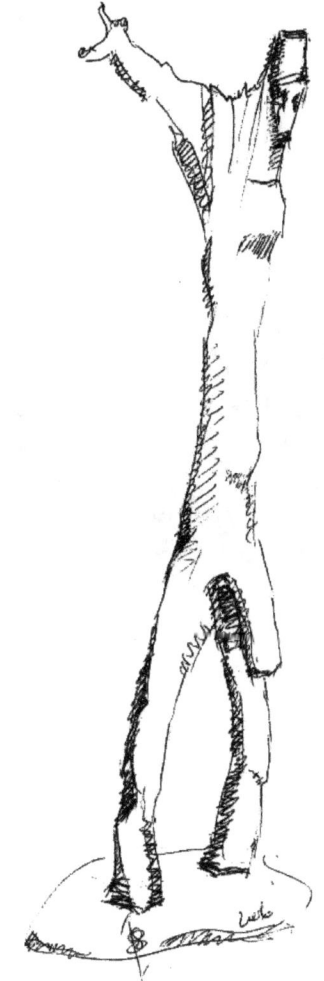

FONTOM
(COMFORT)

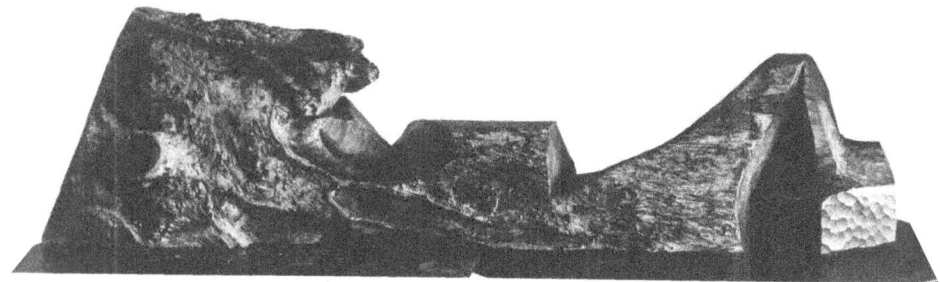

YEAR; 2005
DIMENSION: L150 x H50 x W50CM
MEDIUM: SENNA SIAMEA
COLOUR: BURNT UMBER

Fontom, in Akan literally means *Comfort*. The Akan culture endorses the African philosophy of charity. This philosophy soothes the agonies of the weak and poor through a support system in which the wealthy absorb the financial difficulties of the needy. Based on this belief, the weak and poor, the aged and vulnerable, destitute and insolvent and others are continually maintained by the strong, privileged and generous.

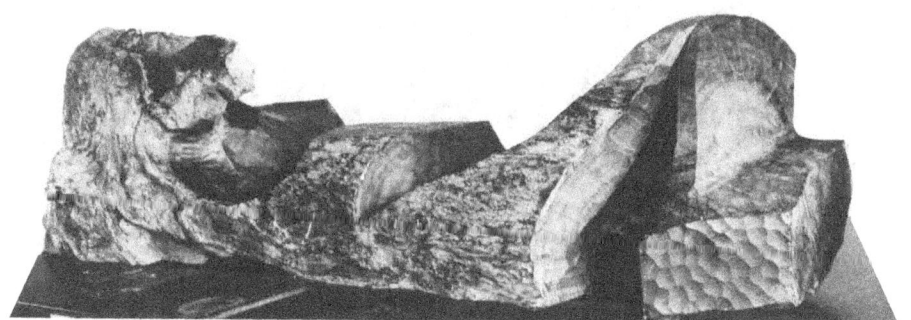

Fontom is a composition of a reclining female figure resting on her back. *Fontom* is produced from a tree trunk that has projection at the top right portion. This projection forms part of the head of the female figure. The figure has both elbows stretched backward. The lower part of the upper arm lies besides the torso and both hands are set across the lower portion of the abdomen.

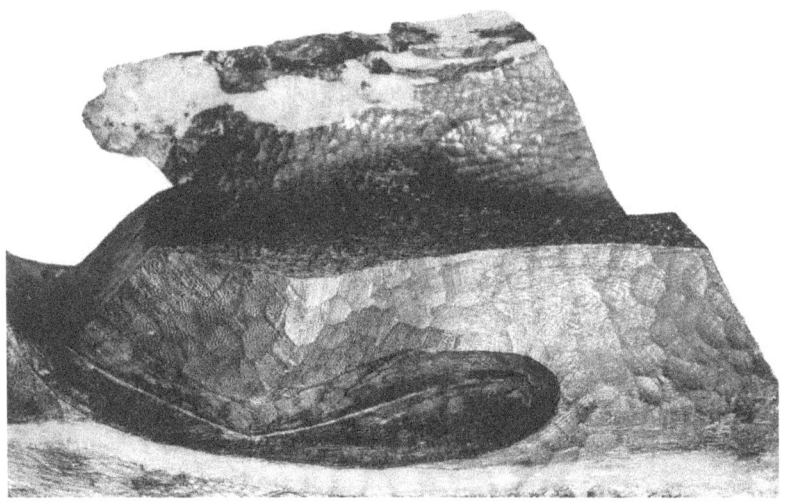

The figure has both knees raised and connected to the foot and buttocks. The foot is bulged. The knees that connect the foot and buttock swing towards the left. The chest of the figure displays fused bulging breasts raised to the level of the hands. Like the breasts, the legs are fused together with the hands. The upper arms have been left uncarved leaving them in the natural tree bark. No detail was rendered to the face, hands, legs and foot. The entire composition makes use of few anatomical details.

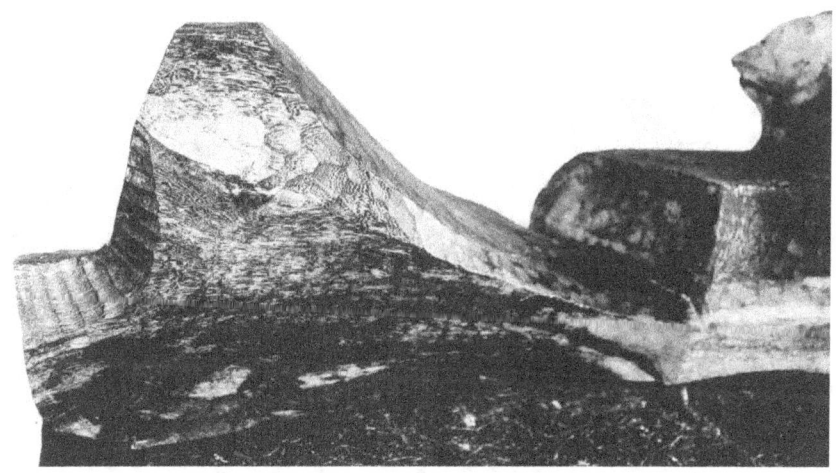

CONCEPT

Fɔntɔm symbolizes the culture of charity, relief and compassion that the Akan people observe to create sanity and comfort in the community. The Akan culture applauds the process of support for one another as the basis for which the needy and the vulnerable are to be assisted by the individual, family and community. Although individuals, families and communities are to a large extent expected to provide for themselves and their dependents the necessary material and psychological needs;

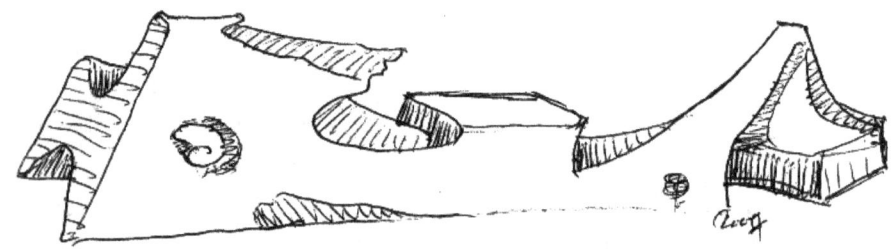

it may also be quite impossible for certain individuals, families and community to provide the necessary needs and support expected of them and their dependants for growth and progress. In Africa everybody is somebody's keeper. The privileged and generous have the moral trust and compassion to assist the weak, poor, aged, vulnerable, destitute, insolvent etc. The reclining pose reflects the period of prolonged silence and relaxation. It also suggests an effective mind exercise, repair of the body and soul and retire from a previous activity as well as a launch into a greater life journey.

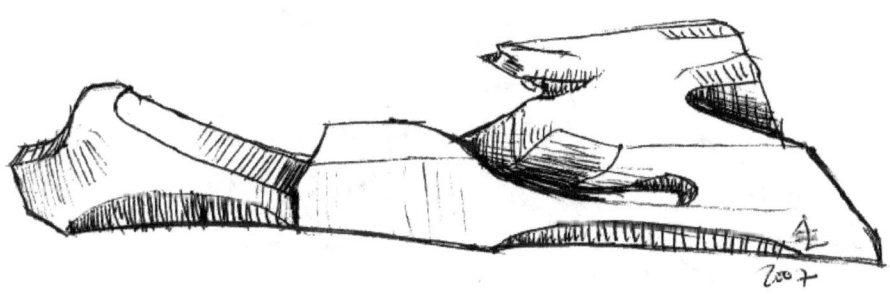

The faceless head connotes a season of the night, fright, dejection and neglect. The faceless head presents to the individuals and communities imageries of hope, prosperity and better future that await the broken hearted, the oppressed, the dejected and the guilty. Like the Akan adage *sum mu wɔ adaaso* literally meaning *darkness fulfils dreams*.

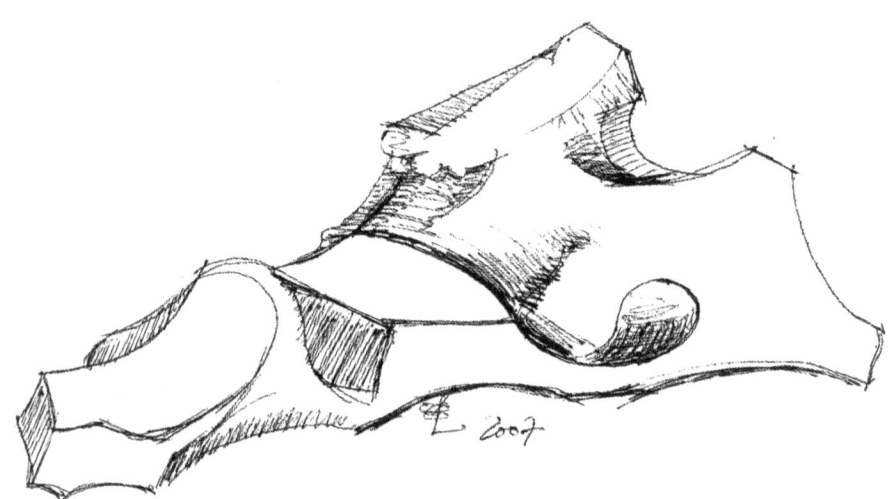

GYAE DEM YƐ
(PUT A STOP TO THAT)

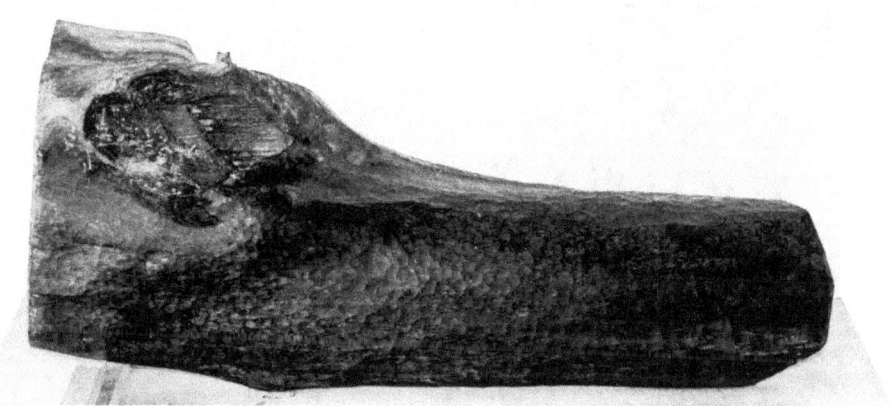

YEAR; 2005
DIMENSION: L120 x H50 x W40CM
MEDIUM: SENNA SIAMEA
COLOUR: BURNT UMBER

Gyae Dɛm Yɛ in Akan literally means *Put a Stop to That*. *Gyae dɛm yɛ* is an Akan corrective deity. Among the Akan people, the belief is that a deity exists to punish all persons who pursue evil and unaccepted behaviour. The prime responsibility of this deity is to prompt deviant persons of their actions and thoughts and offer corrective measures where necessary.

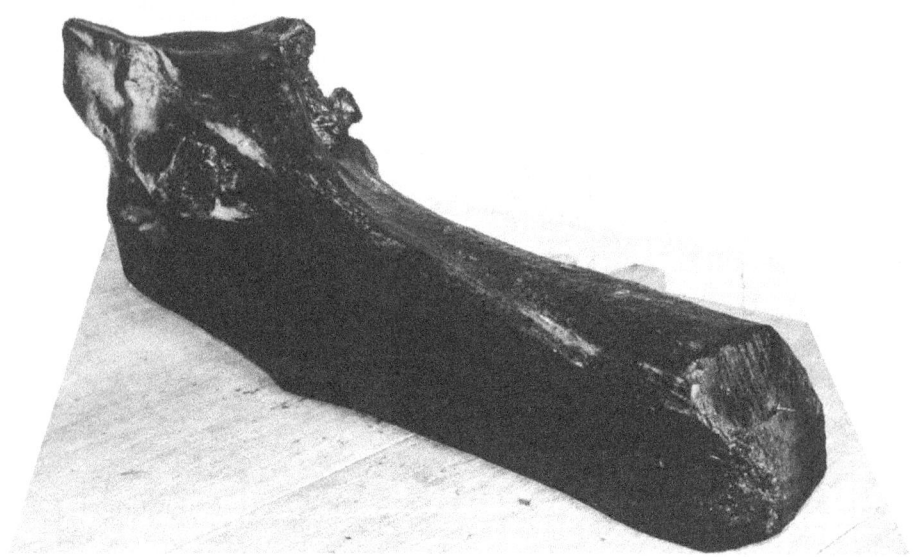

In addition, it corrects the bad to become good. Based on this sanctions and punishments deviant and evil persons undergo reformation possibly to become better and fruitful in order to honour and pacify their loved ones, families and community at large rather than face retribution.

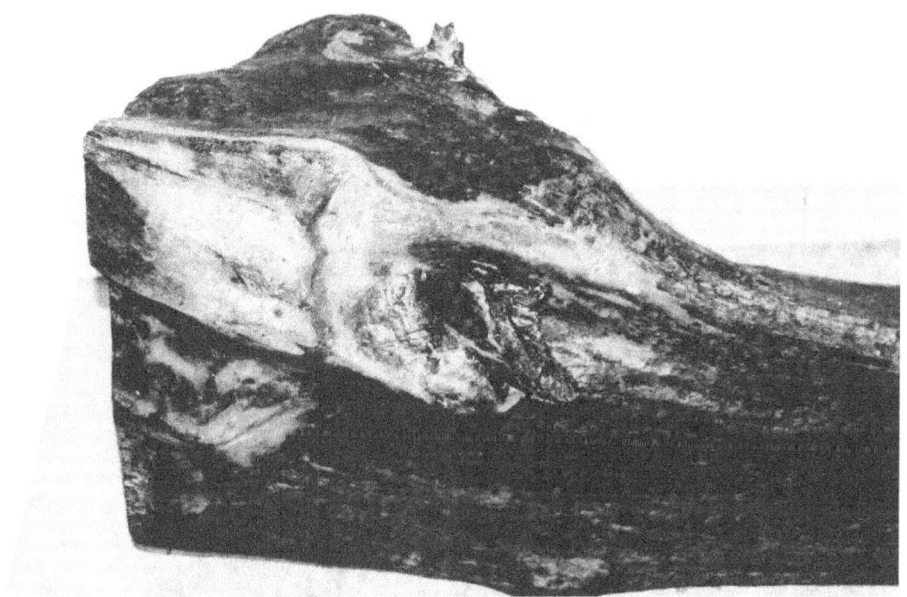

Gyae dɛm yɛ is a composition of an alligator head that has jutting eye balls and closed mouth. The composition is made from a tree trunk that has a bulging part and an elongated portion. The bulging part constitutes the forehead and the eye portions. The eye portion includes the raised sections making up eyebrows, the dual depressions forming the sunken eye sockets and eyeballs produced from separate offshoots. These represent the visual spots of the alligator.

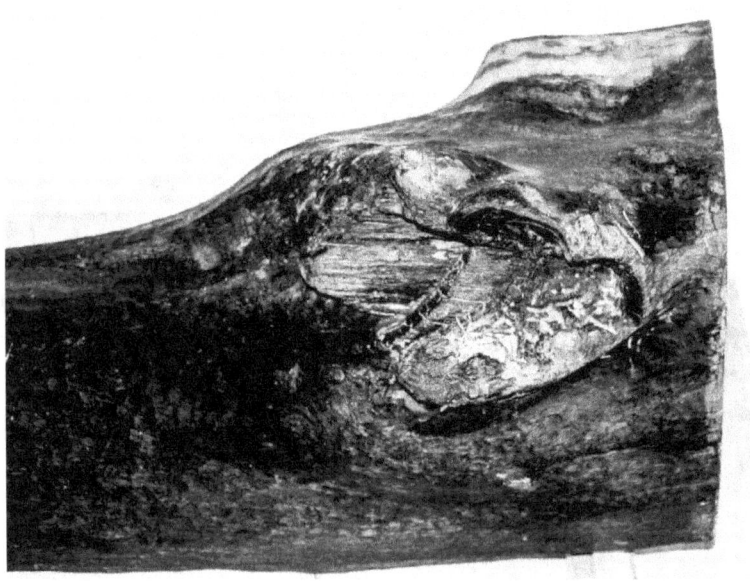

The elongated portion represents the shaft of the alligator's mouth. The deity is seen alert, ready to pounce on persons or community members about to offend or subject persons to terror. She is also prepared to offer instant and effective reforms before such persons become wayward.

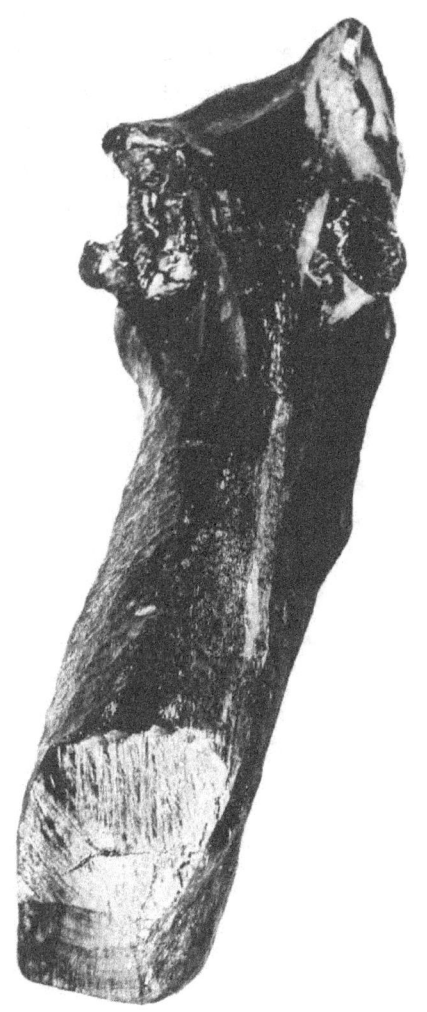

CONCEPT

Gyae dɛm yɛ symbolizes the culture of Akan corrective practice which seeks to build better and fruitful life among community members. The Akan culture offers appreciation to the process of reformation and support for persons who by intent or wrong exposure may become social misfit or negative role model to the family and the community. *Gyae dɛm yɛ* presents an Akan anthropomorphic deity who rewards virtue and punishes vices. She is the symbol of stability, sanity as well as good neighbourliness.

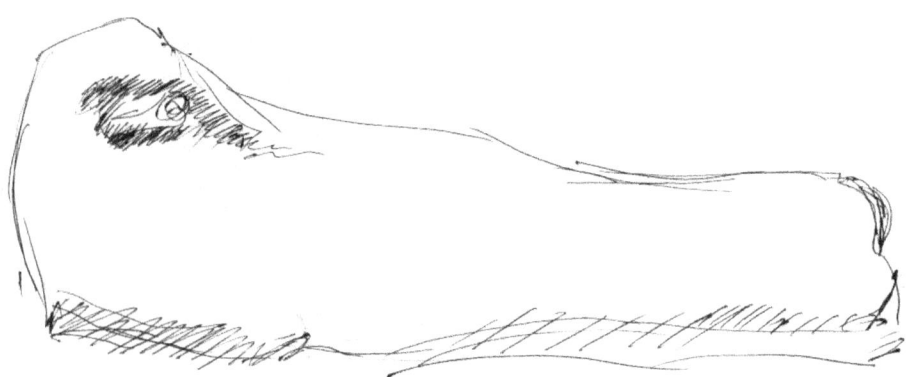

The alligator is that type of animal that can hide from its adversaries and spring surprise on them where necessary. It is an all weather animal that survives both on land and in water body. The alligator, although poor in hearing, possesses a strong and sharp sight similar to that of an eagle. At sight, it is able to quickly coil around its prey with the tongue making it incapacitated.

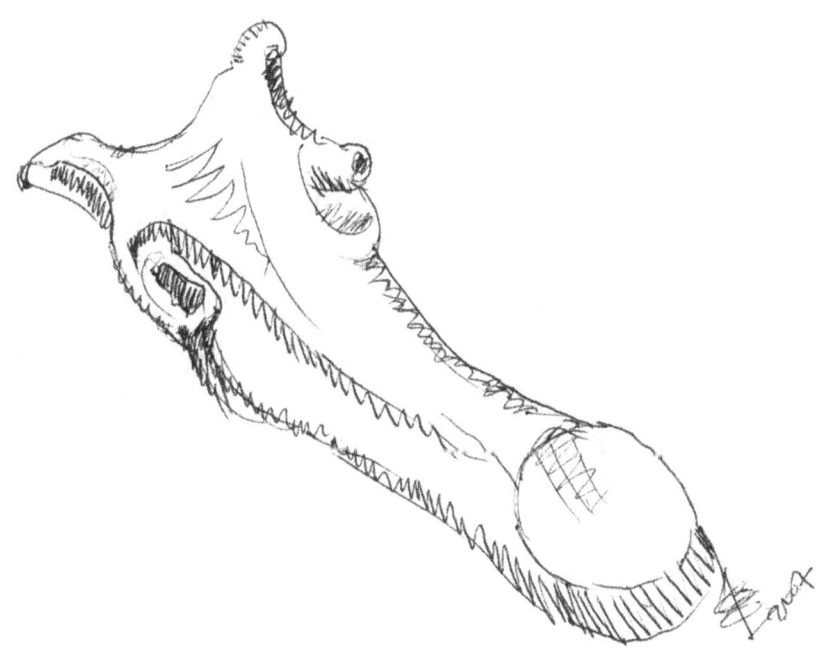

As extremely calm as it is, the alligator is fast pacing and has the capability of subjecting its prey to quick and brutal punishment due to its nature and number of teeth. Therefore, the alligator, a vigilant creature, is capable of retiring an antisocial behaviour and character of persons in the community.

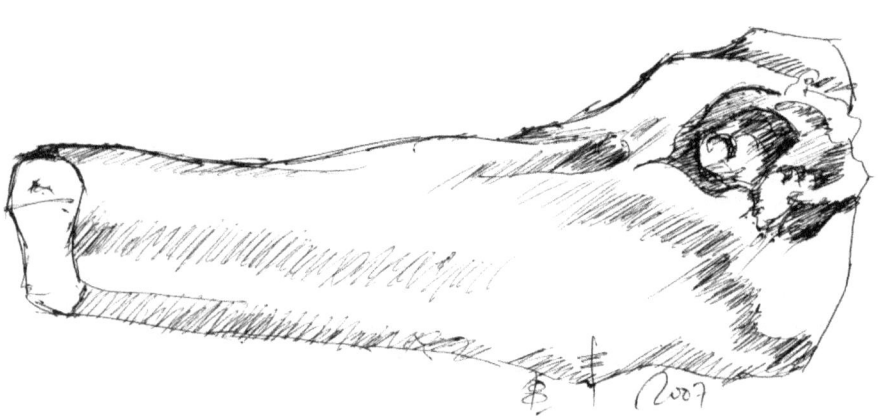

Gyae dɛm yɛ offers to the Akan community the expected security and comfort required of a community. Hence, the Akan adage *sum mu wɔ adaaso* literally meaning *darkness promotes dreams*. It also assures the community the needed peace that may emanate from the sanity of its indigenes. Like the Akan adage *sɛ wɔadandan woa, nna nyimpa nya wo ho mfaso* literally means *a reformed person is an asset to humanity*.

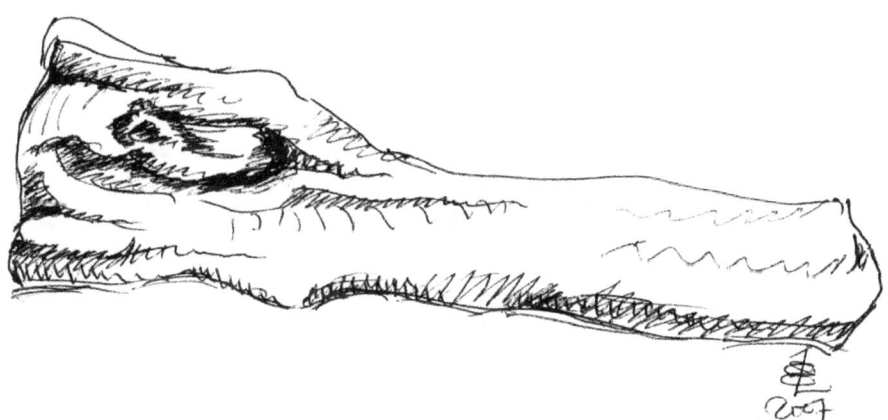

MPAEBƆ
(PRAYER TO THE ANCESTORS)

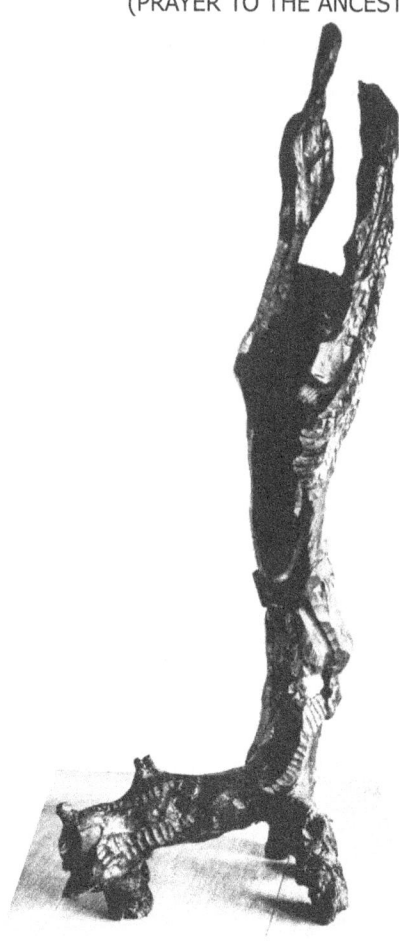

YEAR; 2003
DIMENSION: H220 x L90 x W50cm
MEDIUM: SENNA SIAMEA
COLOUR: JET BLACK

110

Mpaebɔ in Akan literally means *Communicating with a Supernatural Being*. In Akan culture, there is strong belief in the existence of the Almighty God, as the Supreme Being and the creator of the universe. There is also the belief that He created certain supernatural forces who act as mediators between the living and Him. These supernatural forces are deities, ancestors and lesser spirits. To the African, communicating with the Supreme Being requires doing that through the mediators. For this reason, an elderly woman who presumes her journey to the other world offers reverence to her ancestors and asks for directions.

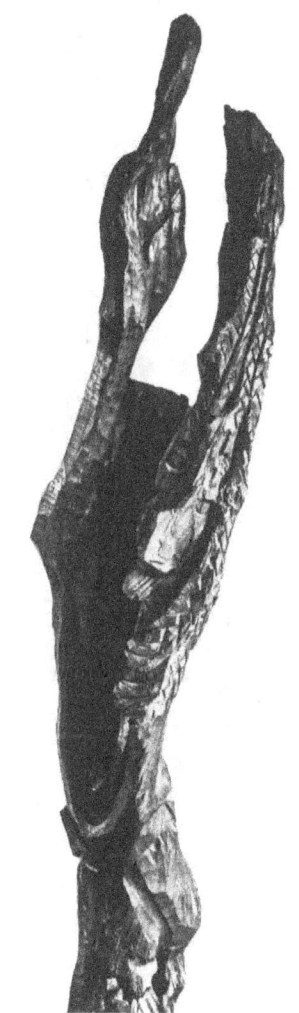

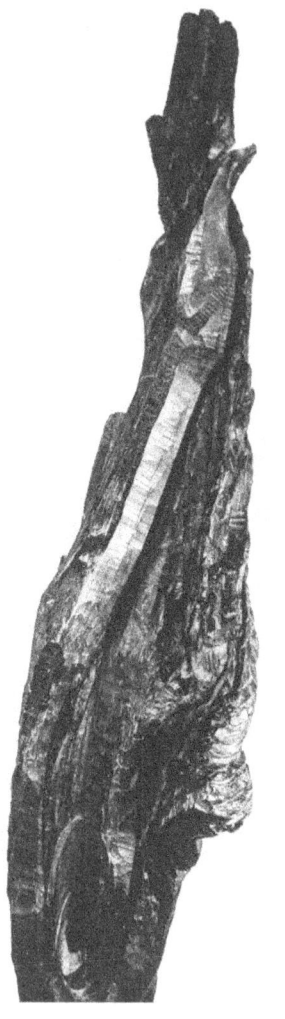

She also renders thanks for their unflinching support all through her life. Therefore, this composition seeks to reiterate this African value of looking up to the creator for support and direction. *Mpaebɔ* is a pole sculpture that has a lateral base. The figure is in a squatting pose but the buttocks are resting on one heel of her foot. The composition reveals the top portion of a female who wears an elongated and elaborate coiffure that is peculiar with African women. The right upper arm of the figure is raised high up while the left that is positioned behind her shows a raised elbow. The upper part of this left arm is bent downwards.

The hand is also turned upwards and assumes a zig-zag rendition. All of these flow along the lines of the coiffure to align with the raised right upper arm. From the front, the coiffure drips towards the chest forming an alignment with the elongated neck that supports the lean and long face. The base of the neck is coiled gradually into the elaborate ornament placed around the neck.

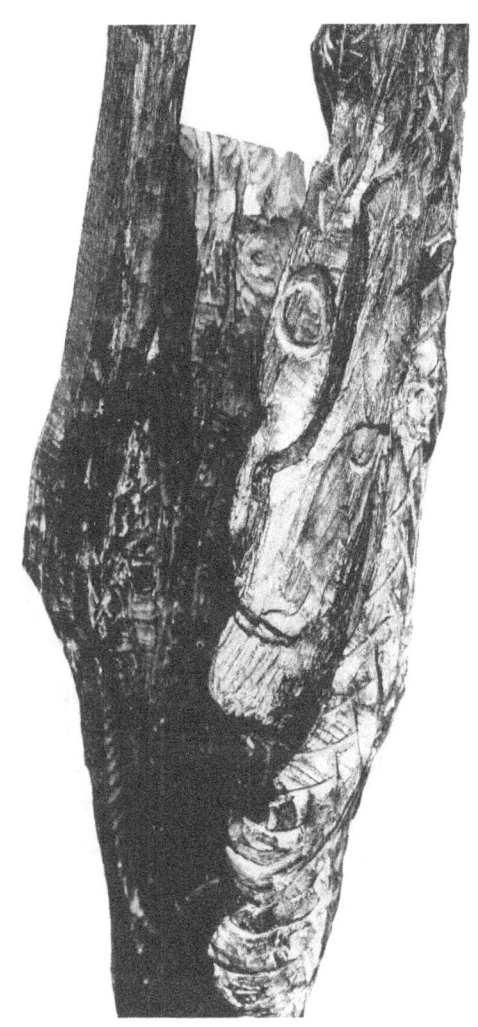

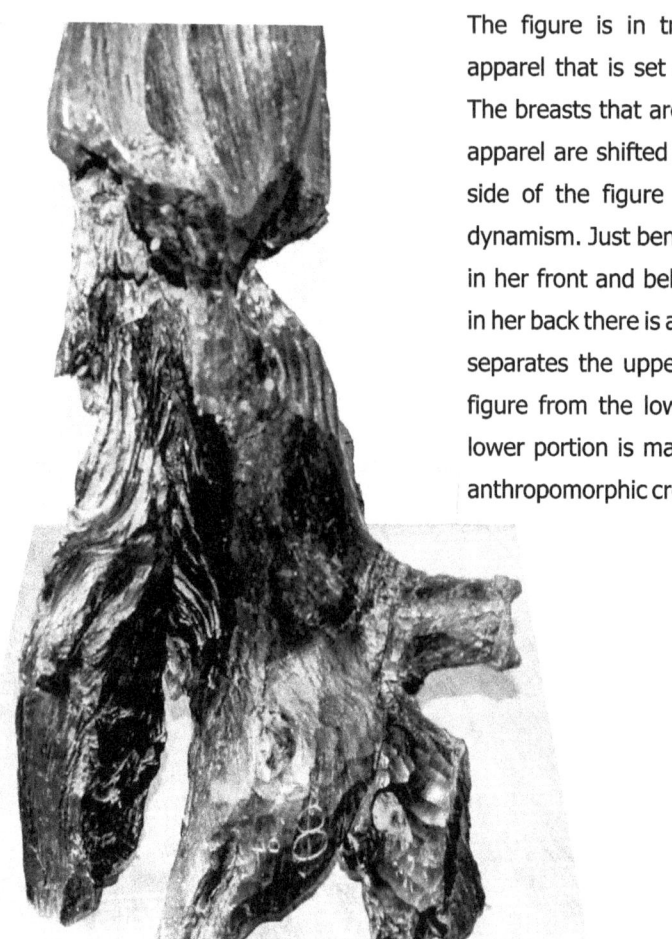

The figure is in traditional casual apparel that is set above the bust. The breasts that are encased in the apparel are shifted towards the left side of the figure to create some dynamism. Just beneath the breasts in her front and below the buttocks in her back there is a perforation that separates the upper portion of the figure from the lower portion. The lower portion is mainly made up of anthropomorphic creatures.

These creatures constitute the base of this composition. They are the outstretched form representing the head of a buffalo, head of a horse, and head of a bird. This is followed by the head of a snake and then the head of a pig. These are presumed to be the spirits that reside in the elderly woman. The entire composition (with the exception of the ends to the projection) is fully carved.

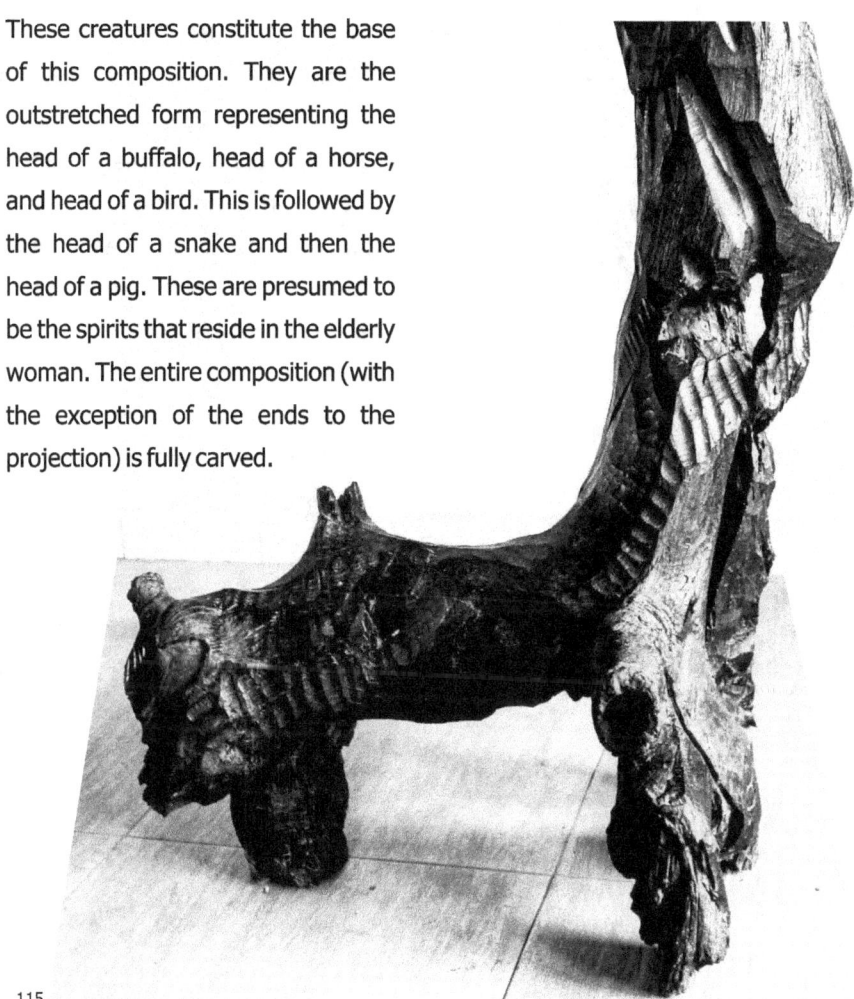

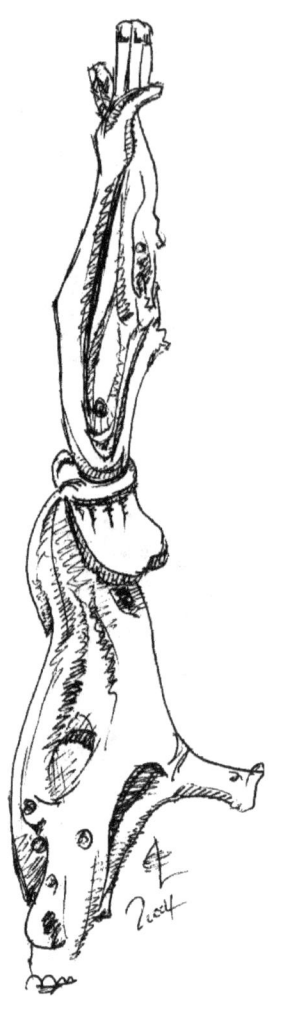

CONCEPT

Mpaebɔ in this concept symbolises the preparation by an elderly person before embarking on the journey to the other world. It is imperative though arguable, to state that most living persons for want of successful lives seek some supernatural forces to help them accomplish their ambitions. These forces which are sometimes referred to as *abayea* or *bayerɛ* are witchcraft spirits and are not accepted in the land of the ancestors. As such, these spirits may be donated to off-springs and siblings or community members to continue with their assignments before their departure from the rightful owners.

In Africa, such spirits are acquired for good and evil. Most persons who acquire these spirits for evil deploy them for destruction. They may be used to deplete the finances of their victims, cause madness, dullness, strange ailments, barrenness, loss of sexual potency and even death. Those who acquire them for good employ them to create wealth, protect children, family and relationship, protect trade and establishment, as well as improve the mental capabilities and alertness of owners and their dependants. Such spirits may be so domineering that they may control the character and physical being of the possessors.

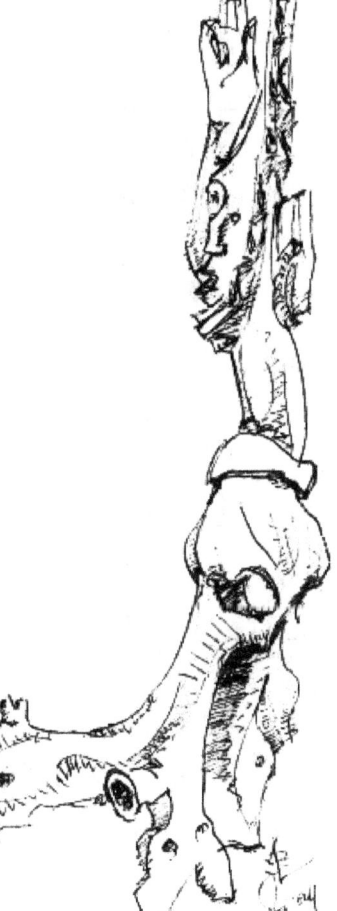

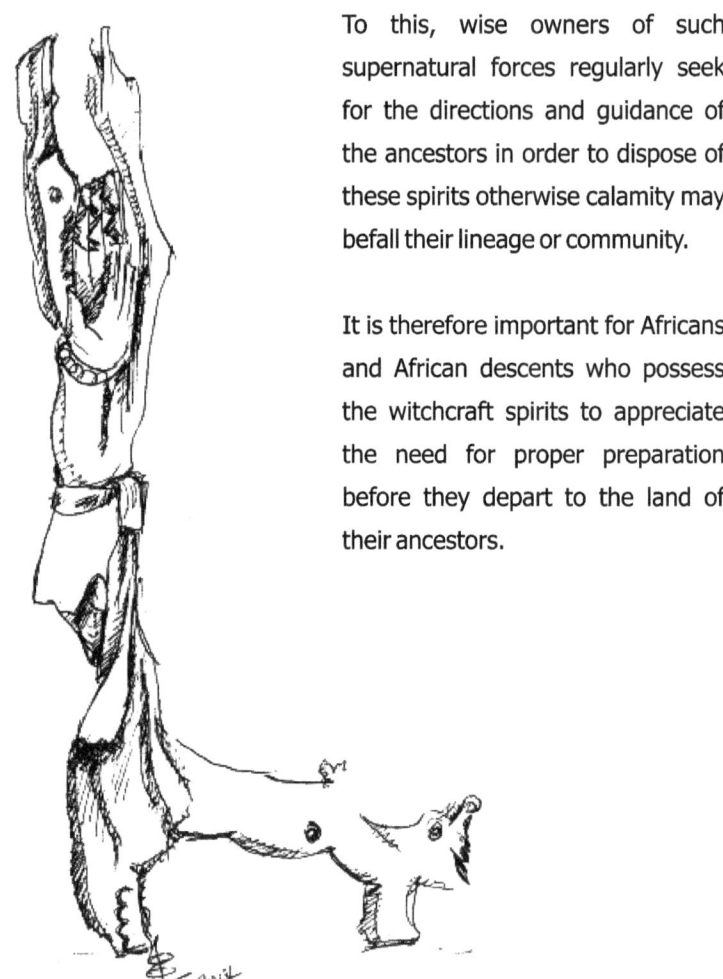

To this, wise owners of such supernatural forces regularly seek for the directions and guidance of the ancestors in order to dispose of these spirits otherwise calamity may befall their lineage or community.

It is therefore important for Africans and African descents who possess the witchcraft spirits to appreciate the need for proper preparation before they depart to the land of their ancestors.

SIKADAM
(CRAVING FOR WEALTH)

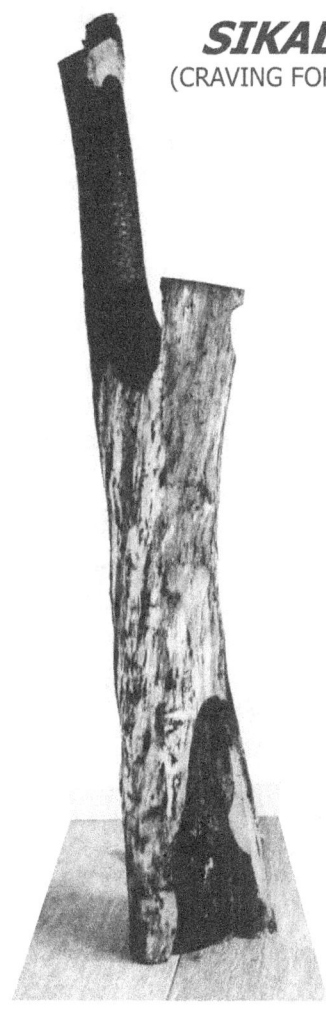

YEAR; 2005
DIMENSION: H195x L30x W30cm
MEDIUM: SENNA SIAMEA WOOD
COLOUR: OFF WHITE &OFF BLACK

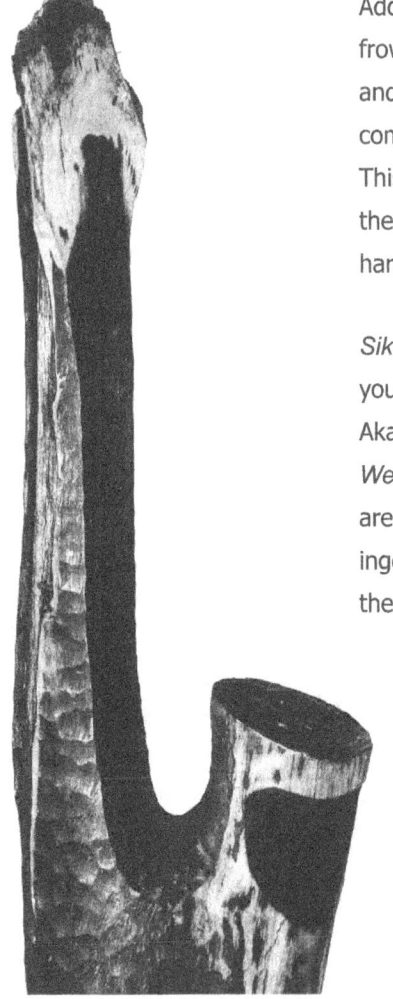

Additionally, the Akan culture totally frowns on corruption, fraud, deceit and greed which have become common among the youth of today. This composition seeks to reiterate the African value of integrity and hard work.

Sikadam is a composition of a youthful male indigene. *Sikadam* in Akan literally means *Craving for Wealth*. In the Akan culture males are expected to be industrious, ingenious and be able to provide their needs through genuine means.

In African culture, punishment is meted out to a young male indigene who amasses wealth using dubious means in the community. It is required of the youth to embrace integrity, hard work, selflessness, dedication, and focus. It is a pole sculpture composed of a twisted tree trunk that has traces of tree sap (bark) portions. The youthful male has firmly raised his right hand. The palm of his hand is opened with tightly fitted fingers that are set in vertical portion as if they are pinned to an item.

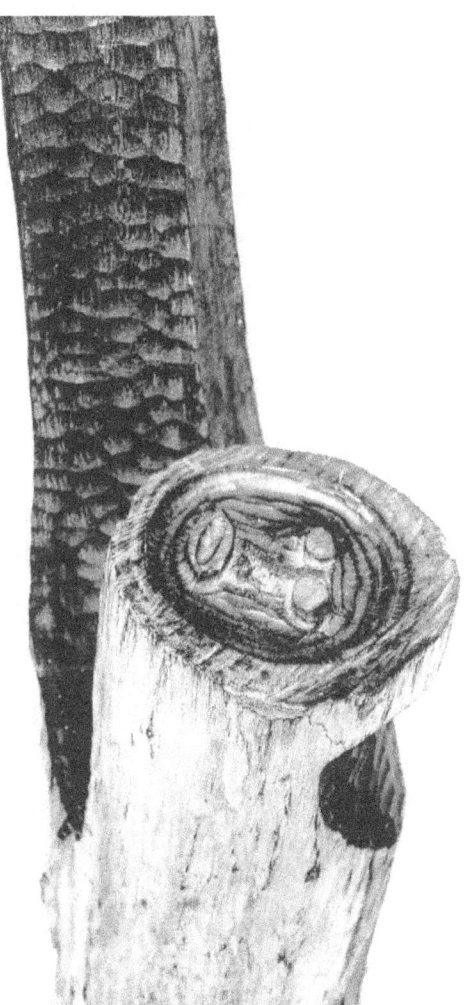

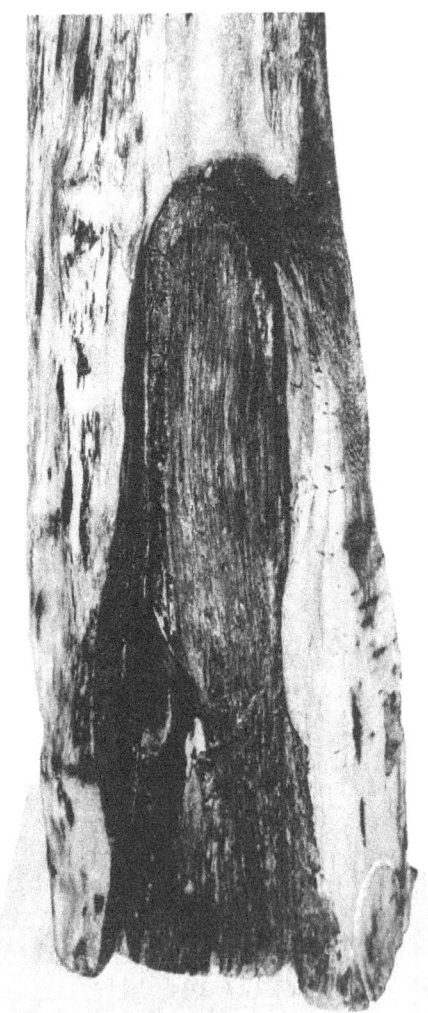

The left hand which is virtually attached to his back right leg has loose fingered palm that stretches downward in a rooted posture. The head of the figure is set at an angle of one hundred and eighty degrees (180^{0}) and has a recessed face directed upwards. The face consists of a wrecked triangular nose that is placed between a set of two bulging nuts representing the eyes and a grooved one standing for the mouth.

CONCEPT

Sikadam preaches the Akan adage that says *dzinpa ye sen ahonya*. This literally means *virtues are better than vices* or *good name is better than riches*. *Sikadam* seeks to inform and educate today's youth on the important principle of life that hinges on integrity, hard work, selflessness, dedication and focus. Much is expected of today's youth to uphold integrity which ensures good attitude, character, honesty, and reliability. Integrity, though difficult to define, forms the personal attribute and hard work which have been outlined as normal effort, extra effort and prudent financial management; selflessness which is a form of declaration to duty, services and dedication to making things happen. Being focused leads to meaningful and purposeful adulthood. This must be the point of call for today's youth.

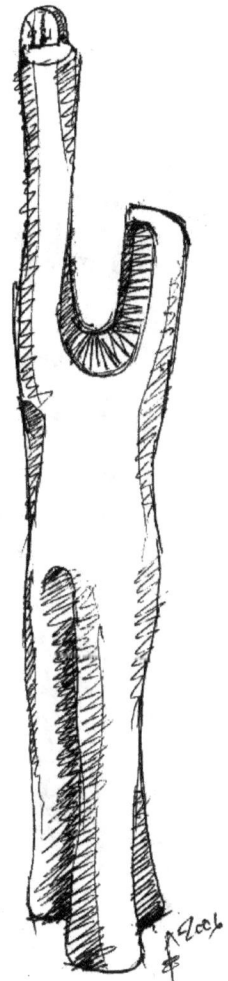

123

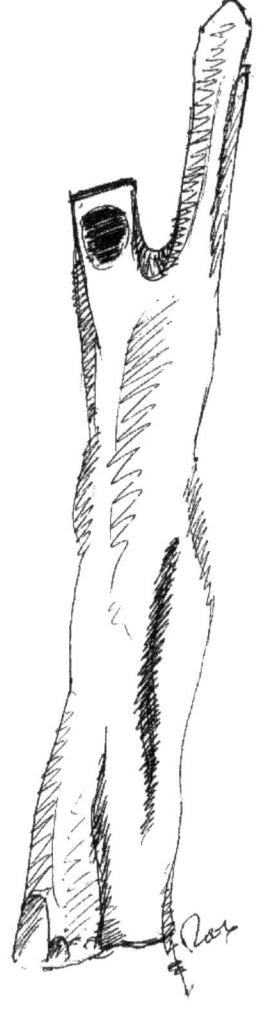

The traces of tree bark and burnt portion of the composition are an indication of the decadence of the indigenes of the community. The bulging nuts representing the two eyes are vehicles capable of perceiving and sensing all things (money and goods) be they desirable or not. The grooved nut represents the opened mouth that depicts an insatiable appetite to consume in a self-centred manner all things belonging to the community. The wrecked nose signifies that the youth are unable to separate good from evil. It is said that a nose that cannot perceive vice from virtue stinks.

In recent times, the youth are said to be the bedrock of today's and tomorrow's success stories. They are perceived to be striving for unsustenable material wealth through greed, fraud and deceit. Sudden success and fast life lead to early death. This situation has become commonplace. 'Let's live and die' has come to replace the adage "good name is better than riches".

The community today gives the pride of place to vices rather than virtues. As a word of advice, today's youth must make a turn to the supreme God for divine direction and guidance in order to abandon the new 'deity of riches'.

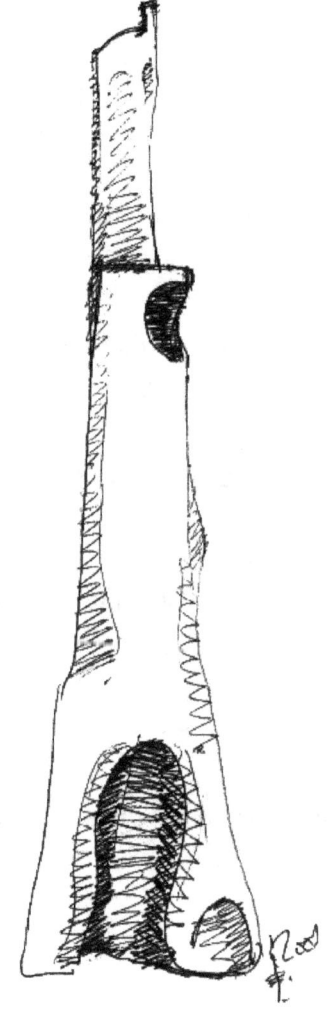

REFERENCES

Every Woman, A Gynaecological Guide For Life: Derek Liewellyn Jones, Faber and Faber Limited, Gt. Britain, 1999.

Inspirations From Nature- Art From The Coast Of Ghana: Patrick Tagoe-Turkson and Sampong Ofori-Anyinam, Dafoko Concepts, Accra, 2013.

Art Across Time (Volume II Edition): Laurie Schneider Adams, McGraw-Hill College, Boston, 1999.

Gilbert Living With Art Core Concepts In Art: Mark Getlein, The Mc-Graw - Hill, London.

Wood Carving: William Wheeter and Chartez H. Hayward, Duke Publication, Sterling Publishing Company, New York, 1979.

Ghana Hardwoods

Sculpture from Antiquity To The Middle Age: Philippe Bruneau, Mario Torelli, Xavier Barreli Alter, Taschen, China, 2006.

Sculpture Today: Judith Collins, Phiadon, London, 2007.

Begin Sculpture: Ronald Unger, Right Way, UK,

Sculpture; Technique, Form and Content A Guide For Teachers: Judith Collins, Phiadon, London, 2007.

Henry Moore From Bones and stones to Sketches and Sculptures: Jane Mylum Gardner, Four Winds Press, New York, 1993.